Dedication

We dedicate this book to our children Alexandra, Michael, Oliver, and Brenner, who inspire us and remind us each day why our goal, and the goal of many families, is to provide our children with the best education possible, now and in the future.

A debt of gratitude is owed to our spouses, Eleanor and Delphine, for their patience, and support of our work and this project.

CONTENTS

Publisher's Note

The examples in this book are provided for informational purposes only and do not reflect the actual performance of any investment. All programs involve investment risk, including the loss of principle. State taxes may also be applicable.

FREQUENTLY ASKED QUESTIONS

1. What is a 529 College Savings Plan?

A 529 College Savings Plan is a *savings plan* established and maintained by a state to assist families who are saving for college expenses. These plans are created under federal law and allow for tax-deferred growth on the investments, as well as federal (and sometimes state) income tax-free withdrawal from the account if the assets are used for *qualified higher education expenses*.

2. How do I open a College Savings Plan account?

Almost every state has a plan either in place or under development. The plan can be accessed via the Internet, or by contacting the state treasurer's office or the financial services firm retained by the state to administer the plan. See the Appendix for state websites that contain addresses, phone numbers, and additional information.

3. What are the benefits of a College Savings Plan?

The College Savings Plan allows for assets to be professionally managed, to appreciate *income tax deferred,* and provide *income tax-free withdrawals* if they are used for qualified higher education expenses.

4. Are there income limits or thresholds that phase out or eliminate the ability to contribute to a College Savings Plan account?

No. There are no income or other limits on the ability to contribute to an account other than the maximum funding level that each state designates for its particular plan.

5. Who can establish a College Savings Plan?

Any person can create a College Savings Plan for any other person or for the benefit of themselves. As long as the assets are withdrawn for use for qualified higher education expenses, the growth on the investments will be federally income tax-free. This creates an opportunity for people to begin saving for possible graduate school or professional school later on in life, and not only for their children's higher education expenses.

6. Once the College Savings Plan account is opened and the beneficiary is named, can we change the beneficiary?

The College Savings Plan account allows for the change of beneficiary at any time by the account owner. Certain beneficiary changes are *income-tax free,* while other changes result in income taxation and a possible penalty tax. Care must be taken in making beneficiary changes.

7. Can the owner of a College Savings Plan account close the account and take back all of the money?

Yes. The owner of a College Savings Plan account can withdraw all of the funds in an account at any time. However, this will lead to income taxation on the earnings on the account, as well as a *10% penalty* for withdrawing the funds and not using them for qualified higher education expenses.

8. Who is allowed to be a beneficiary?

Any person can be a beneficiary, whether it is a related person (such as a child, grandchild, or spouse) or someone who is not related. The beneficiary must be a US citizen or a resident alien. You can also establish the account for yourself as the beneficiary.

9. Once an account is established, who has control over the investment decisions?

Each Plan Manager develops a number of model portfolios in which you can choose to invest your savings. Federal law requires that the consumer have *no control* over investment choices. As such, Plan Managers have provided a large number of options for the consumer to select from.

10. Can anyone contribute to a 529 account maintained for a beneficiary?

Each state's plan is slightly different. However, as a general rule, most 529 plans allow for any person to make contributions into an existing 529 account.

11. What are the most common investment options given by Plan Managers?

A common investment offering is the *age-based allocation investments,* which are geared towards your child's age and the year in which he or she will attend college. There are also asset allocation investments, growth investments, aggressive and conservative investments, as well as a variety of equity and fixed income options within most plans.

12. Can you change investment options once they have been selected for the College Savings Plan account?

The investment option chosen for a College Savings Plan account can only be changed once every twelve months. However, each time a new contribution is made to a College Savings Plan account, a different election can be made with respect to how these newly contributed assets are to be invested.

13. Is there a federal deduction for contributing to a College Savings Plan?

No. At the present time, there is no federal deduction for contributions to a College Savings Plan.

14. Are there state deductions for contributions to a College Savings Plan?

Yes. Many states have laws allowing for a full or partial deduction on personal income tax returns for contributions made to College Savings Plans.

15. **Are the withdrawals from a College Savings Plan free from federal income tax?**

A withdrawal from a College Savings Plan is free of federal income tax if the proceeds are used for *qualified higher education expenses* at an accredited institution. Generally, these schools are accredited if they participate in the Federal Student Aid Program. You can contact the Plan Manager for the state in which the school is located or contact the school directly to determine whether they meet this standard.

16. **Are withdrawals for College Savings Plans free from state income tax?**

Withdrawals from a College Savings Plan may be taxed to you depending on your state of residency. Many states have adopted the same tax rule as under federal law and exclude these plan proceeds from income tax. As such, these states will not tax distributions. Other states do not have their own income tax, and again, they would not be taxing distributions. Still other states have state income taxes and have not adopted federal law, in which case these states will tax distributions from a College Savings Plan account.

17. **Can the College Savings Plan assets be used for all colleges and universities?**

The College Savings Plan assets can be used for *most* accredited institutions of higher education in the United States. Generally, those schools— whether college, graduate, vocational, or trade school—that participate in the Federal Student Aid

Program are eligible for participation in the College Savings Plan.

18. How do you change the beneficiary on a College Savings Plan account?

Each Plan Manager will maintain their own forms for purposes of updating beneficiaries on accounts. A *change of beneficiary* form can be completed to reflect a new beneficiary.

19. Does the changing of a beneficiary generate an income tax?

The relationship of the new beneficiary to the old beneficiary may determine whether there is an income tax, penalty tax, or gift tax on the change of beneficiary.

20. Can I borrow money from the plan or use the plan as security for a loan?

No. Federal law specifically states that you cannot use the account as collateral for a loan or borrow money from the plan.

21. What happens if money is withdrawn from the plan and not used for qualified higher education expenses?

When assets are withdrawn from the plan and not used for *qualified higher education expenses*, an income tax (federal and state) must be paid by the owner. He or she must also pay a 10% federal penalty on the income.

22. **Who will own my account if I pass away before the account is fully utilized?**

Under the existing ownership rules, an account owner has the ability to name a successor owner on the account. If no successor owner is named, then the owner's *Last Will and Testament* will determine who the new owner will be.

23. **How does the College Savings Plan affect qualification for financial aid?**

Under existing rules, a College Savings Plan account will be treated as an asset of the owner and not an asset of the beneficiary. For this reason, care should be given to structuring ownership of the College Savings Plan account to be certain it minimizes its impact on obtaining financial aid.

24. **What are *Upromise* and *BabyMint,* and how do they relate to a College Savings Plan?**

Upromise and *BabyMint* are membership programs that offer *free* contributions from corporations with whom consumers do business. *Upromise* is also a 529 Plan Program Manager. These corporations provide contributions to a College Savings Plan account of a participant who purchases their goods.

25. **Are College Savings Plan accounts taxed to the owner if the owner should die?**

The College Savings Plan account is not taxed to the owner should the owner pass away while retaining control of it, unless the owner had made a large gift and was prorating the annual gift tax exclusion over a number of years, and died during that term of years.

26. Can the College Savings Plan account be obtained through an employer and be deducted from payroll?

Yes. College Savings Plan accounts are becoming a popular voluntary corporate benefit. It affords the employee the same College Savings Plan opportunity at a lower cost and allows for the use of payroll deduction. Much like the popularity of the 401(k) benefit, a College Savings Plan that is obtained through an employer is more likely to be used by the employee than if they had to secure such an account on their own. The College Savings Plan, as a voluntary employee benefit that utilizes payroll deduction, enhances the likelihood that people will save on a periodic basis for college expenses.

27. What happens if the beneficiary of a College Savings Plan account chooses not to go to college?

A College Savings Plan allows for the owner of the account to change the beneficiary of the account at any time. Making this change is as simple as signing a change of beneficiary form with the Plan Manager. Depending on the blood relationship of the original beneficiary to the new beneficiary, the change of beneficiary may be a tax-free change. In some circumstances, if the new beneficiary is not *a member of the family* of the old beneficiary, then the owner may be subject to income taxes and a penalty tax.

28. Must I use the College Savings Plan for the state in which I reside or my beneficiary resides?

There is no requirement that you must use the College Savings Plan offered by your home state (or the home state of you beneficiary). However, there may be income tax reasons for using your home state plan rather than a plan offered by another state. These tax reasons can include some form of possible income tax deduction at the time of contribution, or state tax-free withdrawal at the time funds are used for qualifying higher education expenses. Some states have taken steps to impose an income tax on funds withdrawn from a College Savings Plan maintained with a state other than your home state even if the funds are used for qualifying higher education expenses as a way to encourage you to use your home state's plan.

29. Does the College Savings Plan *sunset* at the end of 2010?

Yes. Under current federal tax law, the College Savings Plan is scheduled to *sunset* (come to an end) on December 31, 2010. By the very nature of the sunset law, Code Section 529 will cease to exist after that date and these College Savings Plans will no longer be given favorable tax benefits on earnings. This may result in these accounts being subjected to income tax and possibly the penalty tax. However, commentators have discussed this issue at length and generally concur that it is *unlikely* that the sunset provision will be left in place.

30. Can I establish a College Savings Plan for myself and/or my spouse?

Depending on your state's plan, you may be able to establish a College Savings Plan account for yourself or your spouse. If you or your spouse decide to go to college, those funds can be used for education expenses. You can also begin saving for a child who has not yet been born, in an effort to begin the tax deferred savings afforded by the College Savings Plan. In addition, funding an account for yourself in anticipation of a grandchild as a wealth transfer tool may be a reasonable estate planning opportunity.

31. Can a person be a beneficiary of more than one College Savings Plan?

Yes. A person can be beneficiary of as many College Savings Plans as he or she likes. Each state's plan mandates a maximum funding level. However, there is no requirement that all of a particular beneficiary's plans be in one state.

32. Can one beneficiary have College Savings Plans in more than one state and fund each plan to its maximum level?

Yes. Under existing law, there is no prohibition against funding as many College Savings Plans as you would like to the maximum level for the beneficiary. However, this tactic is likely to raise scrutiny from the IRS and may be treated as tax evasion—not an appropriate College Savings technique.

33. **If the owner of a College Savings Plan account needs nursing home care, will the College Savings Plan account be lost to the nursing home expense?**

The simple answer is that there is no clear answer yet. Once a gift is made into a College Savings Account, the money in the account should no longer be available for the owner's debts and expenses. Unfortunately, the issue of whether money in a College Savings Plan account can be lost to the owners' nursing home expenses is based on state law. Each state has its own rules as to what assets will be available for nursing home expenses.

34. **What happens if a state does not renew its contract with a Plan Manager?**

Each Plan Manager has a contract with the host state to provide 529 product services. These contracts can be of any length, but are typically five years or more. As these contracts come up for renewal, some states will elect to make changes, thereby impacting the 529 Plan investments. In some cases, the existing Plan Manager will be allowed to retain the plan assets for some period of time.

In other circumstances, the investments in the Plan Manager's 529 offerings will be transferred into the new Plan Manager's similar type of offerings. This raises concerns for the consumer who specifically selected a plan based upon its Plan Manager. In circumstances where a program manager is replaced, the consumer will be left with the choice of staying with the state's program with a new Plan Manager, or in the alternative, rollover the plan assets to another state where their preferred Plan Manager has a program. Caution must be exercised though, as the rollover to another state's plan may be treated as a taxable event in your home state. It may also cause the recapture of a state income tax deduction that was granted at the time of contribution to the account.

35. Does it make sense to have more than one 529 Plan account for the same beneficiary?

There are times when it does make sense to have several accounts for one beneficiary. The most notable reason is to maximize possible state income tax deductions. For instance, if you reside in a state that gives a limited benefit for contributions to the state's plan, you may wish to contribute the amount necessary to fully use the income tax deduction to the state plan. You may wish to invest the balance of your college savings into a different 529 Plan that might have more preferable investment options or better performance, fees, and expenses.

36. Is there a difference between a 529 Plan purchased through an advisor and a 529 Plan that is purchased directly from the Program Manager or the sponsoring state?

The only difference between plans sold through an advisor and those purchased directly is the level of advice that you will receive. The cost of the advice from a financial advisor is the *load fee* of such plans. The benefit of the advisor is that you will have someone to help you select the 529 Plan best suited for your family, considering all factors (such as years remaining until college, state income tax benefits, risk tolerance). Some states only offer plans through a financial advisor and some offer only direct sold plans, while other states offer both advisor and direct sold plans.

37. **Can I close an existing custodial account for a child (UGMA/UTMA accounts) and use the assets to open a 529 Plan?**

Yes, custodial accounts can be changed into 529 Plan accounts. The 529 Plan must be a custodial type of plan so that the child (as represented by the custodian) remains the rightful owner of the account. You cannot take custodial account assets and use them to open a 529 Plan that does not reflect the custodial nature of the account.

38. **To move assets from a custodial account to a 529 Plan, must the custodial account assets be sold?**

To transfer an existing custodial account into a 529 Plan custodial account, you must first sell all of the assets in the custodial account. Plans can only receive cash, so all custodial account investments must be liquidated. This may result in an income tax or capital gains tax on the custodial account assets.

39. **Does a gift into a 529 Plan account incur a gift tax?**

Special gift tax rules allow for an individual to make a tax free gift into a 529 Plan of $11,000 per person, per year ($22,000 for married couples) to

as many people as they like. You can even acceler-
ate these gifts by making five years' worth of gifts
($55,000 per person, or $110,000 for married couple)
all at once.

40. Should I open and maintain one College Savings Plan for all of my children (or other beneficiaries), or should I open a separate account for each child?

It is possible to open and maintain one College
Savings Plan account for all children/beneficiaries
you may have, although only one person can be
named as beneficiary of the College Savings Plan
at one time. If you have only one account for mul-
tiple beneficiaries, then you will need to be certain
that after the first person uses funds for college,
the name of the beneficiary is changed to the next
beneficiary who will use funds for college. It is
often preferable to have separate accounts for each
beneficiary as a way to ensure that investments in
the account are properly tailored for each individual's age, as well as to provide a separate account
for family members and friends to make gifts to.

1

THE BASICS OF 529 PLANS

Few things can keep a parent awake at night like the seemingly ominous task of saving for a child's college education. Thanks to recent actions by Congress, saving for college has become slightly easier. Internal Revenue Code Section 529 has created the single greatest savings opportunity in many years.

Internal Revenue Code Section 529

Internal Revenue Code Section 529 is a newly created tax law that allows each state to create its own Prepaid Tuition Plan and/or College Savings Plan. (To be consistent throughout this work, we will call the governing law *Section 529*.) Congress designed these new plans to help people save money for future college expenses. The idea behind these plans is to be certain that money saved for college is not subjected to tax during the time it is saved or the accumulation stage. This way, families can attempt to keep pace with college costs without the additional, ever-increasing burden of taxes.

The *Prepaid Tuition Plan*—one of two new plans created by Section 529—is established by each individual state. It allows for the purchase of *tuition credits* (like class credits when attending college) for use at participating colleges typically within the state's borders. These credits are held until the child attends college, and are then redeemed for the number of credits purchased. Regardless of how much more the tuition is at the time of redemption, if the credits are used at a participating educational institution, the credits purchased long ago are used as full payment of the current tuition.

EXAMPLE

In 2005, Mary opened a prepaid tuition account as established by her state, New Hampshire, for the benefit of her son, Phillip (age 12). Mary purchased 8 semesters of credits (4 years) and paid the tuition expense of $40,000 ($5,000 per semester). In 2011, when Phillip begins attending college (one that is affiliated with the plan), the first semester's tuition expense is $8,000. When the funds are used to pay tuition, the credits originally purchased for $5,000 satisfy in full the total tuition cost of $8,000. No income is recognized by the IRS as income for tax purposes, so no one needs to include any income on his or her tax return for the $3,000 *appreciation* (difference) on the tuition credits.

Since the Prepaid Tuition Plan affords little flexibility in terms of other financial planning opportunities, little will be mentioned in this book on these plans. Rather, the focus will be on the *College Savings Accounts* (or *529 Accounts*, as they have become known). They are also commonly referred to as *529 Plans*. (All three names refer to the same concept.)

While the law creating these College Savings Accounts is simple in nature, the application is anything but simple for the consumer. There are many reasons for this, none as important as the state-by-state differences among the plans. The law creating 529 Accounts allows each state to develop its own version, and create limitations, tax benefits, funding limits, rules, and regulations as it may choose. As long as a particular state's program meets the basic Internal Revenue Service (IRS) criteria for being a 529 Plan, the consumer will not be subjected to any tax on the investment gains while the assets are growing. The consumer will be able to take money out tax-free if used for *qualified higher education expenses*, as provided by Section 529.

EXAMPLE

In 2005, Joan opened a College Savings Account as established by the State of Maryland (and administered by T. Rowe Price) for the benefit of her son, Steve (age 12). The initial deposit was $20,000. In 2011, when Steve begins attending college, there will be a total of $35,000 in the College Savings Account. When the funds are used to pay tuition, a portion of each payment is made up of the income earned on the investment (the $15,000 appreciation). If the College Savings Account is used for tuition, room, board, etc., then no one needs to include any income on their tax return. The $15,000 appreciation completely avoids all forms of taxation.

Plan Managers

The College Savings Account is an investment account managed by a state treasurer or a financial service firm selected by the state. At the time of this publication, there are more than 30 institutional providers of a College Savings Account (529 Plans) of one form or another. Firms presently participating include many of the investment and mutual fund companies widely recognized across the country, such as:

- Fidelity Investments;
- Putnam;
- T. Rowe Price;
- TIAA/CREF;
- Salomon Smith Barney;
- ManuLife;
- MFS;
- State Street;
- Merrill Lynch; and,
- Alliance Capital.

Throughout this book we will refer to these investment houses as the *Plan Manager*.

It makes sense that an *institutional approach* (removing the management of the investments from the individual to the professional) to these investments will be more efficient than allowing each person to self-direct his or her investments (a 401(k) or IRA). Only time will tell if the institutional investor will be able to live up to this goal.

Getting Started

Establishing a College Savings Account is as simple as completing an application with one of the Plan Managers. Completing the application and getting started is relatively simple. Much like any financial investment, there are many different choices available for investing the assets. You must give thought to the duration, risk tolerance, and available investment options within the College Savings Account before you settle on an investment strategy.

> **NOTE:** Due to the complexity of investing in the College Savings Plan, we strongly suggest that you obtain advice from a qualified financial advisor.

Rules, Rules, Rules

The law is clear as to what is required of each state and of the consumer to achieve the benefits of tax-free growth on investments. To qualify for special tax treatment, federal tax law requires that the account must meet the following basic requirements.

- The account must be created under a state's 529 Plan.
- The account may only receive cash contributions—no stocks, securities, or other business interests.
- No one—whether the owner, contributor, or beneficiary of the account—can have investment control over the account. Only the state—or its delegated investment firm—may direct the investments.

- Only certain maximum levels of funding are allowed.
- The College Savings Account cannot be pledged as collateral or security.
- The program, as administered by the states, must provide a separate accounting for each beneficiary of a plan.
- The College Savings Account *must* be used for *qualified higher education expenses.*
- The College Savings Account funds *must* be used at an *eligible educational institution* to have all gains and appreciation be tax-free at the time of distribution.

The Account must be Created Under a State's 529 Plan

By requiring each state to adopt its own plan (rather than a uniform national plan), each state can tailor and modify the plan as it sees fit. This will allow for changes and improvements as the years go on.

While the industry is still in its infancy, differences among the states have started to occur and changes are being adopted on a frequent basis. Understanding the differences among these state plans, when coupled with the many investment options and the returns on the account assets, can help a well-informed consumer select the appropriate College Savings Account. It can also confuse the consumer who, without a professional advisor, may wander aimlessly among the options. This may result in an inability to even get started opening an account.

Differences Among the Plans

Some College Savings Accounts are only available to those who reside in the state. Some plans are available to non-residents, but only through a broker—who typically will charge a sales commission or an annual fee during the period of time the assets are invested in the plan.

Each state has its own rules about whether a resident investing in his or her state's plan gets a special income tax deduction. In addition, each state has its own rules about whether the withdrawal of funds from an account will be income tax-free or taxable at the time of withdrawal.

Some plans have enrollment fees, an annual account maintenance fee, asset-based management fees, and an underlying fund expense. These fees are often in addition to that which is paid to the advisor assisting in the opening of the College Savings Account.

There are also differences stemming from the choice of investment options (or lack of options). Some plans have investment choices based on the consumer's preference or tolerance for risk (*e.g.,* growth, balanced, aggressive growth, bond fund) and exposure to the marketplace. To gain a competitive edge, the Plan Managers continue to increase the consumer's options in an effort to give them some measure of control over the selection of investments.

The Account may only Receive Cash Contributions

Under the law creating College Savings Plans, it is absolutely clear that only cash can be used to open or contribute to a College Savings Plan. This seemingly innocent requirement does create an issue for those who have been saving for college for some time now. For many years, the traditional approach to saving for college has been to utilize an account titled in the child's name under the *Uniform Gift to Minors Act* (UGMA) or its more modern relative, the *Uniform Transfers to Minors Act* (UTMA).

Governed by individual state's laws, these UGMA/UTMA savings accounts are taxable investment accounts, with all taxable income taxed to the child. Under these *kiddie tax* laws, income and capital gains of a child under 14 are taxable to the parents, and after age 14, are taxable to the child. Certainly, those with existing accounts will seek a way to transfer the existing account into a College Savings Account.

Unfortunately, the UGMA/UTMA account is normally not invested in cash, and would require that all the investments in the account be sold and converted to cash before the money could be transferred to a College Savings Plan. This *liquidation* would result in taxable income if the account had *appreciated* (gone up) in value.

You cannot have Investment Control Over the Account

Only the state or its Plan Manager (the designated investment firm) may direct the actual investments of the account, while the owner, contributor, or beneficiary of the account cannot. For the consumer, this means that there is a loss of control over the investing of assets. For many, this may be the best possible thing. For others, it will create a frustration over seemingly lost opportunities.

To provide more flexibility to the consumer without violating this mandate, the Plan Managers have begun offering more than just *age-based* investment options. Many Plan Managers now allow for *risk-adjusted* options within these age-based approaches.

When a College Savings Account is opened, the person who opens the account is very often labeled the *owner*. The owner is the person who has the ability to name the *beneficiary*, change the beneficiary from time to time, and withdraw funds from the account. While being prohibited from having direct control over investments, the account owner can gain some measure of control by searching for a Plan Manager that provides the options that meet with the account owner's liking.

Given that the many Plan Managers will each have their own selection of funds and alternative investment options, account owners may look for opportunities to *chase* the best return in the marketplace. (Chase means to try to time the market by jumping in and out of investments.) To prevent an account owner from gaining control (indirectly) of the investments by shifting from one Plan Manager to another, the law prohibits the transfer of an account more than once per year.

EXAMPLE

In 2005, Maye opened a College Savings Plan as established by New Hampshire for the benefit of Sean, age 12. Maye invested in the Plan Manager's Age-Based 2013 Fund. After one year, she grew frustrated over the fund's performance and decided to move the account to another Plan Manager administering a

continued...

different state's College Savings Account. In doing so, she selected a more aggressive investment option, which was more suited to her liking. The transfer to the new plan does not violate the rules and does not create any income tax consequence for Maye or Sean.

Only Certain Maximum Levels of Funding are Allowed

Remember, these plans are designed for the purpose of saving for college. Parents can save for children; grandparents for grandchildren; charities can save for scholarships; aunts, uncles—everyone can save for everyone, but not too much. Even as expensive as college is, there is a limit. The law only allows for the saving of money for *qualified higher education expenses*. Since the law allows each state to implement its own sets of rules, this is one area that will vary from state to state. As you compare state-by-state plans, you can see differences in the maximum funding level.

For instance, in 2003 in the state of Rhode Island, the maximum funding level was $301,550, while in New Hampshire the maximum was $250,000. Most states are close in total maximum funding, being somewhere in the $250,000 to $300,00 range. In reviewing the participation handbooks for the various Plan Managers, you can determine the rationale for that particular state.

The way it is supposed to be done (as provided by regulations) is by determining the estimated cost of tuition, fees, and room and board of a student attending five years of undergraduate school at the most expensive school in the state. So you can see that on a state-by-state basis, this amount should not vary much.

The value of fully funding a College Savings Account goes beyond the ability to adequately provide for a child's college education. As a wealth transfer tool, the fully-funded 529 Plan can create substantial estate tax, gift tax, and generation-skipping transfer tax savings for families of wealth.

The College Savings Account cannot be Pledged as Collateral or Security

As a society, we tend to borrow too much, too often. However, the law makes it clear that the 529 Account is not allowed to be used as *collateral* for a loan or other debt. You cannot pledge or borrow against the 529 Plan. This means that the money really will be used for college unless the money is withdrawn. In that case, there would be a *disqualifying distribution.*

By preventing the account owner from borrowing against or pledging the College Savings Account for his or her loans or debts, these assets will truly be *hands-off,* and the assets will grow for college expenses. This puts the consumer in a position of either finding other sources for short-term borrowing or completely withdrawing assets from the College Savings Plan and incurring both the income tax and a 10% penalty on the income withdrawn. Congress' intention was to make this disqualifying distribution a costly exercise to act as a deterrent from short-term borrowing.

The Program must Provide a Separate Accounting for Each Beneficiary of a Plan

It seems obvious, but the law makes it clear nonetheless—a Plan Manager must provide a statement of each beneficiary's account, providing the following details (at least annually):

- contributions during the accounting period;
- account value;
- earnings; and,
- distributions.

Most Plan Managers send a quarterly account statement. The law provides that if the Plan Manager does not send a statement at least annually, they must make the information available upon your request.

The College Savings Account must be Used for Qualified Higher Education Expenses

To get the tax-free investment gains in the 529 Plan at the time of distribution, it is clear that the funds must be for *qualified higher education expenses*. If some or all of the distribution is not used for these qualified expenses, the owner of the account will have to report the portion of the withdrawal that is a gain or profit on his or her tax return. This gain or profit must then be placed on the account owner's tax return and taxed as ordinary income.

In addition, there is a 10% *penalty tax* on the income or gains earned. This penalty acts as a true deterrent for using these assets for anything other than qualified higher education expenses. The basic premise to the plan is that the money saved in this *tax-favored* savings account is intended to be used to pay for college and college-related expenses. (Since the law was first enacted in 1996, the definition of *qualified higher education expenses* has been expanded to include more of what a family would typically expect these expenses to be.)

As amended by the *Economic Growth and Tax Relief Reconciliation Act of 2001* (EGTRRA), Section 529 Plan distributions, including all investment gains and profits, will be completely free of any tax at the time the money is used if it is withdrawn for one or more of the following:

- tuition;
- room and board (if the student is enrolled at least half-time);
- fees;
- books;
- supplies;
- equipment required for enrollment; or,
- for special needs children—expenses incurred in connection with the child's enrollment or attendance at an eligible school. (Congress has not yet defined the term *special needs*.)

The College Savings Account Funds must be Used at an Eligible Educational Institution

Remember that even though the funds in the 529 Plan need to be used for *qualified expenses*, they must also be used at an *eligible educational institution*. The law defines the term *eligible education institution* by means of reference to the *Higher Education Act of 1965*. A simpler definition is that any accredited college, graduate, or post-secondary, trade, or vocational school that can participate in the federal student aid program will qualify. Specific information about a college or university can be found at the following website:

www.ed.gov/offices/OSFAP/Students/apply/search.html

It is absolutely imperative that you verify that the school is accredited and eligible under this definition. You can find out by contacting the school directly or by asking the Plan Manager sponsoring the plan in the state in which the school is located. If the school is not accredited and therefore not eligible, then any distributions from a College Savings Account will be fully taxed to the owner of the account and will be subject to the additional 10% penalty.

Future Changes in the Law

Changes to the law are made on a frequent basis—both to the Internal Revenue Code Section and to any regulations. One item to keep track of is the possibility that the College Savings Plan and its law may *sunset* (come to an end) on December 31, 2010. The *sunset* provision requires additional legislation to keep the College Savings Plan law on the books. Were the law to *sunset* without any changes being implemented, then many of the following will expire on that date:

- tax-free distributions of earnings;
- the ability to rollover plan assets without a change of beneficiary;
- the addition of *first cousin* as a member of the family;
- the ability to contribute to a Coverdell Savings Account in the same year as a contribution is made to a College Savings Account;
- rules about applicability of the College Savings Plan to *special needs* individuals; and,
- the coordination with Hope Scholarships and Lifetime Learning Credits.

While it is unlikely, it is possible that the law will sunset on December 31, 2010. It is unlikely, as recent estimates put the value of College Savings Accounts at approximately $100 billion by the end of this decade. This will represent a substantial portion of the population that is saving funds for college. For this reason, Congress will be hard pressed to reverse the favorable tax benefits given these College Savings Accounts. Nonetheless, if these accounts were no longer to be treated with these favorable tax benefits, then any withdrawal from the accounts, whether used for qualified higher education expenses or not, would be subject to ordinary income tax and possibly the penalty tax of 10%.

2

HELPING SAVE
FOR COLLEGE

Any discussion of saving for college should begin with a
clear understanding of the goals you are trying to achieve.
As most financial and estate planners will tell you, it is
the mere fact that you have a plan that separates you
from the pack. Developing a plan of attack is how to
begin. To do this, you must first calculate the amount
that is needed to put a child through college. For sim-
plicity sake, we will focus our discussion on the use of
College Savings Plan assets for payment of college
expenses. Remember, these College Savings accounts
can be used for payments of expenses at post-secondary
educational institutions that offer credits towards:

- a bachelor's degree;
- an associate's degree;
- a graduate level or professional degree; or,
- another recognized post-secondary credential.

This means that the assets in the College Savings
Plan can be used to pay school expenses whether the
student is attending a community college, a vocational
school, or a graduate school. The assets will also
receive the favorable tax benefits.

The following two tables provide an estimate of costs for several colleges across the country. The first one shows the 2004–2005 school year expenses. The second one indicates the estimated expenses in the 2010–2011 school year. This should give some sense of the current reality that confronts families saving for college expenses.

COST OF COLLEGE
2004-2005 ANNUAL EXPENSES

College	Tuition	Room & Board	Fees, Books & Supplies	Total
Columbia University	$31,500	$9,000	$3,000	$43,500
Harvard University	$31,000	$9,000	$2,000	$42,000
Kansas State University *(non-resident)*	$12,000	$5,100	$3,000	$20,100
Stevens Institute of Technology	$28,000	$9,000	$2,000	$39,000

COST OF COLLEGE
2010-2011 ANNUAL EXPENSES
(ESTIMATED 6% INCREASE)

College	Tuition	Room & Board	Fees, Books & Supplies	Total
Columbia University	$45,000	$13,000	$4,200	$62,000
Harvard University	$44,000	$13,000	$3,000	$60,000
Kansas State University *(non-resident)*	$17,000	$7,200	$4,200	$28,400
Stevens Institute of Technology	$40,000	$13,000	$3,000	$56,000

The sooner a family begins to invest for college, the better. In fact, as the following table illustrates, the sooner you start, the greater the likelihood of reaching the funding levels you need.

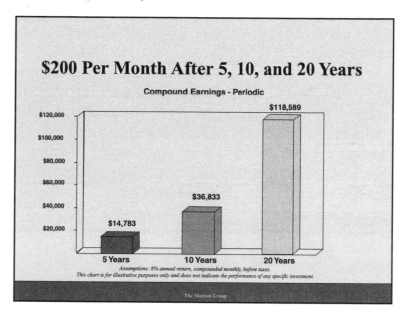

$200 Per Month After 5, 10, and 20 Years

Compound Earnings - Periodic

$118,589

$36,833

$14,783

5 Years   10 Years   20 Years

Assumptions: 8% annual return, compounded monthly, before taxes.
This chart is for illustrative purposes only and does not indicate the performance of any specific investment.

The Morton Group

NOTE: While the College Savings Plan is scheduled to sunset on December 31, 2010, most commentators and planners envision the College Savings Plan extending beyond the possible sunset year.

Taxes and Tax-Deferred Savings

The effect that income taxes have on long-term savings plans can never be understated. The combination of federal and state (where applicable) income taxes can prevent investments from growing as quickly as one would like. The drain that these taxes can have on investment returns can often be substantial. Certainly, the higher the income tax bracket, the more severe the effect income taxes have on the growth of the savings, or *portfolio*. For this reason, it has long been understood that tax-deferred investing is preferred over taxable investing.

Prior to the beginning of the Coverdell Savings Account and the College Savings Plan, the only traditional investments that were tax-deferred were retirement plans (pension plans, profit-sharing plans, defined benefit plans, 401(k)s, individual retirement accounts, etc.) and annuities. Since retirement accounts are intended for retirement, federal laws have established a minimum age of 59½ before withdrawals can be made. This same age rule applies to *annuities* sold by insurance companies. In both cases, the early withdrawal from the account or the annuity will result in some level of income taxation.

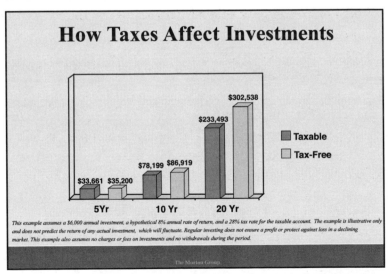

How Taxes Affect Investments

	Taxable	Tax-Free
5Yr	$33,661	$35,200
10 Yr	$78,199	$86,919
20 Yr	$233,493	$302,538

This example assumes a $6,000 annual investment, a hypothetical 8% annual rate of return, and a 28% tax rate for the taxable account. The example is illustrative only and does not predict the return of any actual investment, which will fluctuate. Regular investing does not ensure a profit or protect against loss in a declining market. This example also assumes no charges or fees on investments and no withdrawals during the period.

The Morton Group

The tax deferral opportunity presented by College Savings Plans and Coverdell Savings Accounts, when compared to traditional taxable investments, is substantial. The previous table illustrates the difference on a 5-, 10-, and

20-year timeline when investing tax-deferred versus investing in a taxable account.

It is clear that tax-deferred investing will more often generate a greater pool of assets when compared to the same assets growing in a taxable account.

Other Methods of Saving for College

To truly understand and appreciate the unique opportunity afforded by the College Savings Plan, you should have a working knowledge of the alternative ways to save money for college. Descriptions of the most popular choices follow.

Custodial Accounts

A *custodial account* is one in which a person (the *custodian*) holds money or other investments for the benefit of a person not yet of *full age* and *legal capacity*—usually age 18 or 21. The person who is responsible for holding the assets is known as the *custodian*. These accounts are commonly referred to as *UGMA Accounts* (accounts created under the Uniform Gifts to Minors Act) or as *UTMA Accounts* (accounts created under the Uniform Transfers to Minors Act). In either case, the approach is the same— an account is created for someone who is typically under the age of 18 (or in some cases under the age of 21). The custodian is in charge of all investment decisions, decisions about use of money, and any necessary distributions.

Income earned in these types of accounts is taxable to the child for whom the account is established. Under the *kiddie tax* rules, all income earned in this type of an account for a child under the age of 14 is taxable to the parent, at the parent's highest income tax bracket. Income earned in these types of accounts are fully taxable to the child—on the child's personal income tax return, at the child's income tax rate—once the child is over the age of 14.

Benefits of a Custodial Account

1. *No loss of control over investments.* The investments are fully under the control of the custodian (typically the parent of the child for whom the account was established). Therefore, the assets can be invested in any type of investment the custodian selects. Certainly, the custodian has a duty to make the assets productive without taking unnecessary risk. However, within the boundaries of reason, the custodian has a fair amount of latitude. The flexibility of investments for these accounts allow a custodian to invest in certificates of deposits, stocks, bonds, real estate, and mutual funds. Typically, the investment latitude does not extend to investments in or the trading of options (buying or selling stocks at a fixed price).

2. *Tax Savings.* Because the child will receive a standard deduction of $800 *and* an itemized deduction of $800, the first $1,600 of income completely escapes any form of taxation at the federal level. This is certainly an advantage over investing these same assets in a taxable joint account owned by the parents. (In cases where the parents invest the assets in a taxable joint account, there is no special $800 standard deduction or $800 itemized deduction to protect these taxable investments.)

3. *Ease of Administration.* Opening and maintaining a UGMA/UTMA custodial account is normally very easy.

There is typically just an account opening form to begin the process. The account is maintained in the same fashion as would any other savings or investment account.

Disadvantages of Custodial Accounts

1. *Mandatory Required Distribution.* The laws of the state that you reside in will require the complete distribution of assets in a UGMA/UTMA custodial account. This happens when the child for whom the account has been established reaches age 18 (or in some cases 21). In either case, this mandatory distribution is the single greatest problem with UGMA/UTMA custodial accounts. To the extent that there are assets left in an account—whether as a result of the child not going to college, or a child receiving a scholarship or other financial aid—the remaining assets must be distributed to the child at the age stipulated by your state's laws. This can be problematic if a child is struggling with alcohol, gambling, or drug abuse.

2. *Custodial Accounts Create Ownership Rights.* Custodial accounts, by their nature, are accounts owned by the child, but under the control of someone else—the custodian. These accounts really do belong to the child. For this reason, any inappropriate use of the money or any steps to make the funds unreachable at the age of distribution is likely to violate state law. This can allow the child to sue or take other legal action against the custodian.

EXAMPLE

Dana creates a UGMA Account under Illinois' laws. The account is for the benefit of her son, Paul, age 9. Allen, Paul's father, is named as the custodian of the account. Under Illinois' laws, the account must be turned over to the child at age 18. When Paul is 17 years old, the account has a total value of $100,000, which Dana and Allen intended to use for Paul's college expense. Unfortunately, Paul is involved with alcohol and drugs, and does not intend to go to college. He is looking forward to his 18th birthday, when Allen will be turning over the UGMA account.

To prevent Paul from getting the money, Allen transfers the entire UGMA Account to an *irrevocable trust* (can never be changed) controlled by Allen himself. The trust provides that all of the assets are for Paul's benefit, but Paul cannot have the principal distributed outright to him until he reaches age 35. This transfer to the trust to gain greater control over the assets may violate the state's UGMA law, as it prevented Paul from gaining control at age 18. Paul's recourse is to file suit against Allen for the wrongful transfer of assets away from Paul's control.

3. *Taxation.* An account that has grown in size will begin to generate income that will be fully taxable to the child (or the parent under the *kiddie tax)*. This taxation on the investment income will stunt the growth of the assets. This taxable nature of the account, when compared to the ability to invest on a

tax-deferred basis, is a true disadvantage of the UGMA/UTMA account.

4. *Estate Taxation.* One side benefit to many gift-giving programs is that the gift, once made, is removed from the gift-giver's estate for estate tax purposes. This means that each time a gift is made into a UGMA/UTMA account, the amount of the gift is no longer taxable to the person making the gift. Unfortunately, this desire to remove the assets from the gift-giver's estate does not always occur. Depending on the formalities of the establishment and maintenance of a UGMA/UTMA custodian account, the funds in the account may be included in the estate of the person who is making the gift and remain fully taxable.

Estate tax and gift tax law are clear. If you make a gift, but then control the gift after having made it, the assets never really leave your ownership and the account is fully taxable in your estate should you pass away. To avoid this problem, the custodian of the account should not be the same person that is making the gifts into the account.

EXAMPLE

Sally creates a UGMA account under Illinois' laws. The account is for the benefit of her son, Mickey, age 9. Sally does not trust George, Mickey's father, to properly handle the investments, so Sally sets up the account and names herself as the custodian. Each year, Sally makes a contribution to the account. Several years later, when the account has grown in size, Sally dies. Since she continued to control the account at her death and was the person making the annual gifts, the account should be included in Sally's taxable estate for estate tax purposes. This could have been avoided if she either named George as the custodian, or if she had remained custodian, had George make the annual gifts.

Coverdell Education Savings Accounts (Education IRA's)

The *Coverdell Education Savings Account* (often referred to as an *Education IRA*) is a savings or investment account into which parents can contribute a maximum of $2,000 per year as of calendar year 2004. The investments have the opportunity to grow tax-deferred. When the funds are withdrawn for qualified education expenses—including primary, secondary, and college expenses—the withdrawals, and all increases and gains in the account, are completely tax-free.

The investments a parent can make in a Coverdell Savings Account are completely under the control of the person who establishes the account. The assets can be invested in the most common of investments, such as stocks, bonds, mutual funds, and certificates of deposit.

For families that can save a maximum of $2,000 per year per child, the Coverdell Savings Account may be the best choice available.

Requirements of a Coverdell Savings Account

To qualify for the establishment and for the right to contribute to a Coverdell Savings Account, there are certain income limitations. A married couple must have an *adjusted gross income* (on their income tax return— Form 1040) of $190,000 or less. As the income grows from $190,000 to $220,000, the ability to contribute to an Education IRA is phased out. For single taxpayers, the income limit is $95,000, being phased out at $110,000. Furthermore, contributions for a given tax year must be made on or before April 15th of the following year.

NOTE: Assets in the Coverdell Savings Account (Education IRA) must be used for qualified education expenses (including qualified elementary and secondary school expenses, as well as college and graduate school). It may instead be rolled over to another beneficiary before the original beneficiary turns age 30.

EXAMPLE

In 2005, Nicole (who is single and has an adjusted gross income of $60,000) establishes a Coverdell Savings Account for the benefit of her son, Andrew, age 15. Andrew ends up attending college, but not until he is age 25. He graduates from college at age 29, with $600 remaining in the Coverdell Education Savings Account. Nicole can name her second son, Jay, age 14,

continued...

attending a private high school, as the beneficiary of the account and avoid any penalty for failure to use the account assets before Andrew turns age 30. Now Jay can withdraw the funds in the account, and if used for qualified education expenses, any gain on the assets will be completely tax-free.

Benefits of a Coverdell Savings Account

1. *No Loss of Control Over Investments.* The investments are fully under the control of the creator of the account (typically the parent of the child for whom the account was established). As such, the assets are invested in any type of investment the owner selects. Certainly, there is a duty to make the investments grow without taking unnecessary risk, but within the boundaries of reason, the owner has a fair amount of latitude. The flexibility of investments for these accounts allows the owner to invest in certificates of deposits, stocks, bonds, real estate, and mutual funds. (These investments can contain some amount of risk, including loss of principle.) Typically, the investment latitude does not extend to investments in or the trading of options.

2. *Contributions Can Be Made by Anyone.* As long as the person making the contribution meets the income tests, he or she can contribute to an existing Education IRA for the benefit of anyone he or she chooses—provided the beneficiary is under age 18. An exception to this age limitation exists for *special needs individuals,* for whom contributions can be made even after age 18.

3. *Tax Deferral/Tax-Free Withdrawal.* Much like the benefits of investing within a qualified retirement plan, an individual retirement account, a 401(k), or a College Savings Account, the assets in a Coverdell Savings Account grow on a tax-deferred basis. If the assets are used for qualified education expenses (including primary and secondary education expenses) all gains are completely tax-free.

4. *Ease of Administration.* Opening and maintaining a Coverdell Savings Account are normally very easy tasks. There is typically an account opening form to begin the process. The account is then maintained in the same fashion as would any other savings or investment account.

5. *Account Transferability.* The Education IRA is transferable. A parent can transfer the account to another child should the child for whom it was originally established elect not to attend college or not utilize all of the assets for college.

Disadvantages of Coverdell Savings Accounts
1. *Mandatory Required Distribution.* The law mandates that all assets in the account be utilized before the original beneficiary's 30th birthday. The law does allow for the naming of a new beneficiary, but this age restriction of the original beneficiary continues to apply.

2. *Income Limitations on Funding.* By limiting the ability to contribute to an Education IRA based upon a person's earnings (adjusted gross income), the Education IRA discriminates against those who earn higher income.

It *phases out* the benefit of the Education IRA based upon certain adjusted income levels. When a family's income exceeds the allowable amount, the Education IRA and its benefits are no longer allowed.

3. *Contribution Limitations.* Because the contribution limit is currently $2,000 per year, it will be difficult to grow the substantial funds necessary to satisfy the anticipated expense of college. In addition, some families may qualify for the funding of a Coverdell Savings Account in the early years of saving for college, but not qualify—due to adjusted gross income limitations—in later years. This will limit the pool of assets growing in the account.

4. *Gift/Estate Taxes.* The assets in a Coverdell Savings Account are considered the assets of the account owner. For this reason, there is no completed gift to remove the assets from the owners estate. Therefore, the full value of the account will be included in the taxable estate of the account owner should he or she die while the account is funded.

Prepaid Tuition Plans

The *Prepaid Tuition Plan* allows for the purchase of tuition credits (like class credits when attending college) for use at participating colleges, typically within a particular state's borders. These credits are held until the child attends college and are then redeemed for the number of credits purchased. Regardless of how much more the tuition is at the time of redemption, the credits purchased previously are used as full payment of the current tuition. However, the credits *must* be used at a participating college.

The Independent 529 Plan

The Independent 529 Plan was introduced to the consumer in 2003 as the first 529 prepaid plan solely designed to help finance *private college education.* Prior to this time, all prepaid plans had been created by individual states for colleges within their state's borders. The Independent 529 Plan is a collaboration of over 200 private colleges throughout the United States. Similar to other 529 prepaid plans, the Independent 529 Plan allows for the purchase of certificates that can be used to pay future tuition costs. The program is sponsored by the Tuition Plan Consortium, LLC, and is managed by TIAA/CREF Tuition Financing, Inc.

Much like other prepaid plans, in the event the beneficiary does not attend one of the participating schools, the program allows for a refund of contributions. The refund amount is the amount paid for the tuition certificates adjusted by the net investment performance of the program, with a maximum gain or loss of 2% per year. If the amount refunded is not used for qualified higher education expenses, then the earnings portion will be subjected to federal and perhaps state income tax, as well as the 10% federal penalty.

Benefits of a Prepaid Tuition Plan

1. *Guarantee of Sufficient Savings.* The Prepaid Tuition Plan affords the owner the guarantee that the number of credits purchased will be redeemed for the same number of fully paid credits when the child attends college. This is a substantial advantage over traditional savings for college. The fluctuations in investment returns and the increasing cost of education may keep the savings from being sufficient when needed. By purchasing

a guarantee (as the Prepaid Tuition Plan affords), the account owner has eliminated a large risk factor in saving sufficient funds for college.

2. *Contributions can be made by anyone.* Any person can purchase Prepaid Tuition for the benefit of anyone they choose.

3. *Tax-Deferral/Tax-Free Withdrawal.* Much like the benefits of investing within a qualified retirement plan, an individual retirement account, or a College Savings Plan, the Prepaid Tuition Plan assets grow on a tax-deferred basis. If the tuition plan assets are used for qualified higher education expenses, then all gains are completely tax-free.

4. *Ease of Administration.* Purchasing the Prepaid Tuition Plan credits is a relatively simple matter. Most states have established these accounts with financial services institutions to make the purchase a simple transaction.

Disadvantages of Prepaid Tuition Plans

1. *Typically Applies to Schools Within the State.* Many states establish the plans in coordination with the higher education institutions in that state. Since the premise is that the cost of a college credit can be quantified today and purchased today for use in the future, the state needs to have a good estimate of these costs. For this reason, most states limit the use of the prepaid tuition to schools within the state.

2. *Fixed or Low Rates of Return.* Students may wish to attend schools in other states. Therefore, most Prepaid

Tuition Plans have a formula for calculating the amount to be returned to the owner should the student elect to attend school at an institution that does not honor the credits, or in a state that does not meet with the terms of the plan. Often, the amount of interest paid on these refunded prepaid tuition plan dollars is very small.

3. *Penalty for Nonqualified Withdrawal.* Most plans impose a penalty should the Prepaid Tuition Plan be terminated for use other than for qualified higher education expenses.

4. *Financial Aid Issues.* Prepaid Tuition Plans are treated as an asset owned by the student. They therefore count as a fully available asset when considering the student's finances for financial aid (similar to the treatment of Coverdell Accounts and UGMA/UTMA Accounts). 529 College Savings Plans are treated differently than Prepaid Tuition Plans, as they are treated as an asset of the owner of the account—typically, a parent. As a general rule, a parent's assets are factored in at approximately a 6% usable rate, a substantial difference than the prepaid impact. Legislation has been presented to Congress to alter this discrepancy between the prepaid plan and savings plan, but as of the date of this publication, no such change has been enacted.

Private/Family Created College Savings Trusts

Traditionally, there have been several commonly used forms of *irrevocable trusts* (trusts that, once created, can never be changed again) used for the purpose of saving funds for college. In general, parents or grandparents would meet with their estate planner to discuss the use of some form of a trust to receive and manage assets being saved for college. In every case where an irrevocable (unchangeable) trust was put in place, the person making the gift transfers the assets into the irrevocable trust. Once the assets were in the trust, the person who made the gift no longer had any form of control over the assets. Furthermore, there was no ability to change a beneficiary of the trust or expand the class of people who might benefit from the trust's assets. A description of some versions of the irrevocable trust follows.

Section 2503(c) trusts

The *Section 2503(c) trust,* a trust specially created by tax law, allows for the saving of assets in an irrevocable trust, with all income earned being kept in the trust. The trust pays all income tax on the earnings at the trust's income tax rate. By virtue of tax law changes a number of years ago, the income tax on a trust's income is very high after a modest level of income has been earned. When the child attains age 21, the *trustee* (the person in charge of following the rules of the trust) must distribute the remaining trust assets outright to the child. This age 21 termination, along with the high level of income tax, has caused these types of trust to fall out of favor as a means to save for college.

Section 2503(b) trusts

The *Section 2503(b) trust,* another trust created by law, allows for the saving of assets in an irrevocable trust, with all income earned being distributed to the child. The child pays all income tax on the earnings at the child's or parents' income tax rate, depending on the age of the child. When the child reaches age 25, the trustee must distribute the remaining trust assets outright to the child. This age 25 termination, along with the high level of income tax until the child reaches age 14 (the *kiddie tax* issues) has caused these types of trusts to fall out of favor as a means to saving for college.

Crummey Trusts

Crummey irrevocable trusts allow for greater control over the principal of the trust for a longer period of time. In these types of trusts, the creator of the trust can stipulate at the time of creation how old a child must be to receive the trust principal. The problem with this type of trust is that the child must receive notice of each gift of assets to the trust, and the child is afforded a certain amount of time (typically not less than 30 days) to remove the gift from the trust. The assets that do remain in the trust are typically taxed to the trust at the trust's very high income tax rates. Required notification at the time of each gift, along with the high income tax burden on these trusts, have caused these types of trusts to fall out of favor as a means for saving for college.

The College Savings Plan Advantage

The key to the College Savings Plan is that the investments and savings grow without having any tax imposed on them. This type of investment without taxation is often referred to as *tax-deferred investing*. Regardless of what tax is or is not imposed at the time the money is withdrawn, the growth on the investments during all of the years prior to withdrawal is on this tax-deferred basis.

The advantages of tax-deferred growth are substantial. No matter what tax bracket you are in, you may achieve greater savings when you do not have to reduce your gains by an income tax (federal and state).

Unlike the traditional savings plan—in which all income earned is taxed in the year the income is generated—with the College Savings Plan, you have the potential to grow the money that would have been sent to the tax collector.

Taking advantage of tax-deferred growth whenever possible makes great investment sense. This is the very same reason many people try to fully fund their retirement plans (individual retirement accounts, 401(k)s, etc.), taking advantage of the tax-deferred growth on their investments afforded by the qualified retirement plan. This tax-deferred growth is the very same reason that the College Savings Plan, with its tax-deferred growth, provides a wonderful advantage to a family trying to save and grow assets for college.

The College Savings Plan also allows for an unprecedented amount of control by the creator of the account over the eventual use of the assets. While direct control over the nature of the investments is prohibited, the owner or creator has control over when the assets are used and for whom they are used. This provides substantial estate planning opportunities that previously had not existed. The ability to change the beneficiary allows for the redirection of assets from one beneficiary to another if the assets are not needed or are not used for college. This also allows for saving money for college before children are even born, or to save for grandchildren that are years away from being born.

Drawbacks

Even though it would appear that the 529 College Savings Plan may be the best choice for investing money being saved for college, there are several potential drawbacks. While the Plan Managers seem to be adding investment offerings on a daily basis, there is a more restrictive pool of investment choices than you would have with other types of savings vehicles.

In addition, should your college savings account lose value, you will not be able to sell the assets and take a capital loss. There are limited circumstances in which you can take an itemized deduction, but you can only do so in years when you completely liquidate your account.

Lastly, the *Hope and Lifetime Learning Credits* (education credits), which afford a tax credit to families who meet certain income levels, must be taken into consideration in your planning. Recent tax laws allow for the education credits to be taken in a year when withdrawals are made from a 529 Plan for the very same beneficiary. If the 529 Plan withdrawals are made and used for the same expenses as the education credits, the withdrawal from the Section 529 Plan will not be tax-free.

3

TAXATION OF COLLEGE SAVINGS PLANS

The College Savings Plan is a creation of federal tax law—specifically, Internal Revenue Code Section 529. As with all tax laws, the legislative intention is to motivate people in a particular way by providing tax benefits. The College Savings Plan is no different. The intention in creating the law was to help families save for college in a tax-favored way. Doing so provides those who are saving for college an advantage over those who do not have children or whose children have already attended college.

Basic Tax Rules

In its simplest terms, if you follow the rules, there are no federal or state income taxes on the investment gains in a College Savings Account during the accumulation or growth of the assets. The investments grow tax-deferred, and if used for the appropriate *qualified higher education expenses*, the growth on the investments will be tax-free.

EXAMPLE

In 2005, Barbara establishes a College Savings Account under the plan administered by New Jersey's Plan Manager. In 2013, when her son Tony attends college, there will be a total of $30,000 in the College Savings Account. This represents Barbara's accumulated contributions of $20,000 and growth of $10,000 on that investment. If the account assets are used by Barbara for Tony's qualified higher education expenses, the $10,000 of growth on the investments will never be subject to federal (and perhaps state) income tax.

When assets are withdrawn from the College Savings Account, there may be a tax depending on the reason the assets are withdrawn and for what they are used. Section 529 imposes a federal income tax, and an additional penalty tax, when the tax-free withdrawal rules are not followed.

Qualified Higher Education Expenses

You must use the funds withdrawn from the College Savings Plan for *qualified higher education expenses* in order to have tax-free investment gains. The basic premise to the plan is that the money saved in this tax-favored savings account is intended to be used to pay for college and college-related expenses. Since the law was first enacted in 1996, the definition of *qualified higher education expenses* has been expanded to include more of what a family would typically expect these expenses to be. Currently, they include:

- tuition;
- room and board (if the student is enrolled at least half-time);
- fees;
- books;
- supplies;
- equipment required for enrollment; and,
- expenses incurred in connection with the child's enrollment or attendance at an eligible school (for special needs children).

This list has been expanding and in the future may well include necessary *incidentals* of attending college, such as an automobile to commute to school.

Eligible Institution

The funds withdrawn from a College Savings Plan must be used for one or more of the previously mentioned educational expenses, and must also be used at an eligible educational institution. An *eligible educational institution* is defined in the *Higher Education Act of 1965* as being a school eligible to participate in a student aid program. Generally speaking, these are accredited schools offering credits towards a bachelor's degree, an associate's degree, and professional, vocational, or other post-secondary education, such as medical school, law school, and pursuit of doctoral degrees.

Taxes on Distributions

By virtue of tax law changes implemented in 2002, distributions from a College Savings Plan are free from federal income tax—provided the distribution is used for payment of *qualified higher education expenses.*

This raises the question of what taxes are to be paid if the withdrawal is not for the higher education expenses. What if a withdrawal is made from the account and the proceeds are used for some other expense? Under current federal tax law, the owner of the account would have to list on his or her income tax return the amount of the distribution that was made up of gains and investment profits. The income portion of this distribution would then be subject to income taxes and a penalty tax.

EXAMPLE

In 2003, Jennifer opened a College Savings Account for the benefit of Scott and deposited $20,000 into the account. At the close of the year (December 31) in 2010, the account value will be $30,000. If Jennifer were to withdraw $7,500 from the account and not use the money for qualified higher education expenses for Scott, a portion of the withdrawal would be subject to federal income tax. The portion is computed based upon the ratio of income to principal in the account. In this case, the proportion is ⅔ principal ⅓ income. Therefore, one-third of the distribution that was not used for qualified higher education would be subject to income tax. In this example, when Jennifer withdrew $7,500 from the account, one-third of the amount, or $2,500, would be put on her income tax return as taxable income.

Deductions for Contributions

Under present law, there is no deduction on your federal income tax return for contributions to a College Savings Plan. While it may be possible that Congress will take this step in the future, there is no indication at the present time that they will do so. Presently, if you wish to save money for retirement, you can also do so on a *pretax basis*. This is done by using a 401(k), IRA, or an employer's pension or profit-sharing plan. These types of plans all allow for you to save money before any income tax is imposed on your earnings. Perhaps Congress will see that this pretax savings would be an opportunity for families trying to save for college, and may some day offer a similar tax-deductible way to put money into a College Savings Account.

Some states have enacted laws that allow for a partial or complete deduction against state income tax for contributions to a state's home plan. That means that for someone living in a state that allows for a deduction, the contribution to a College Savings Plan will reduce their current state income tax burden each year.

To put this in perspective, consider the following illustrations of the value (or lack of value) in the deductibility of a contribution to a state's home plan.

EXAMPLE

In 2005, Megan, residing in Illinois, establishes a College Savings Account for her son under Illinois' Plan Manager (presently *Salomon Smith Barney*). Under the state's income tax rules, there is an unlimited income tax deduction when contributions are

continued...

---

made to the plan sponsored by the state. In this case, if Megan contributed $20,000 to her son's account, there would be a tax savings of $600 ($20,000 times the state's flat income tax rate of 3.0%).

EXAMPLE

In 2005, Sarah, a single individual residing in Mississippi, establishes a College Savings Account for her son under Mississippi's Plan Manager (presently TIAA-CREF). Under the state's income tax rules, there is a limited income tax deduction for contributions up to $10,000 when contributions are made to the plan sponsored by the state. In this case, if Sarah was in the highest tax bracket and she contributed $20,000 to her son's account, there would be a tax savings of $500 (maximum benefit level of $10,000 times the state's income tax rate of 5.0%).

EXAMPLE

In 2005, Sheridan, a single individual residing in Massachusetts, establishes a College Savings Account under Massachusetts' Plan Manager (presently Fidelity Investments). Under the state's income tax rules, there is no income tax deduction for contributions made to a College Savings Account. In this case, Sheridan would receive no state income tax benefit for contributions to the account.

You can see that states that offer a state tax deduction for contributions to a College Savings Account save real money for consumers. This is achieved by allowing families to invest money in a College Savings Plan and reducing their current taxable income by the amount of the contribution.

This is why it is important to understand the state income tax benefit—if any—for each particular state. When a state provides a valuable tax benefit to use the state's own plan, the consumer needs to determine the actual economic value/benefit of doing so. As with any investment decision, there are many factors to consider when selecting an appropriate College Savings Plan. Thought must be given to the issue of state income tax deductibility for contributions. Also, consider investment performance among the plans, fees, and expenses.

EXAMPLE

Linda establishes a College Savings Account for her son under the plan administered by an Illinois Plan Manager. Under the state's income tax rules, there is an unlimited income tax deduction when contributions are made to the plan sponsored by the state. In this case, if Linda contributed $10,000 to her son's account, there would be a tax savings of $300 ($10,000 times the state's flat income tax rate of 3.0%).

If Linda then reviews the investment choices and returns on investment for the plan sponsored by Illinois, she may see that the state's plan has only five investment choices—not the ten or more offered by other states' Plan Managers. In addition, if the Illinois plan is under-performing plans managed by other Plan Managers by a wide margin, she might elect to forgo the state income tax savings and use a plan offered by a different state.

State Taxation on Withdrawals

The federal law is clear. Withdrawals from a College Savings Plan for use in paying *qualified higher education expenses* are income tax-free at the federal level. The same may not be true about taxes that must be paid to the state you reside in.

> **NOTE:** Remember, the College Savings Plan is administered by each state under its own set of rules. As long as the rules the state adopts do not conflict with federal laws, it can establish any rules it likes.

There are many different approaches to state taxation of the College Savings Plan at the time of a withdrawal. The good news is that to the extent there is a tax, the tax burden is charged to the student, at the student's tax rate. The assumption is that the student who is attending college is in a lower income tax bracket than his or her parents.

At the present time, a variety of states offer a tax break at the time of withdrawal—including tax-free withdrawal in some cases—if you use the plan sponsored by your home state. Other states have adopted the federal law, which makes all distributions from the state's plan tax-free for anyone, regardless of state residency. There are still other states that have adopted both their own tax-free laws and the federal laws. This may become important in 2011 when the federal law *sunsets*. The states that have their own tax-free legislation will continue to allow tax-free withdrawals. States that have only adopted the federal law may become taxable withdrawal states when and if the federal law sunsets.

A recent development with respect to state income taxes on 529 Plans relates to rollovers from one state's plan to another. Under Section 529, you are permitted to roll over plan assets for the same beneficiary from one state's 529 Plan to another once in a 12-month period. Even though federal law allows this to be a federal income tax-free event, many states are now beginning to tax participants on rollovers as though the assets in the 529 Plan were liquidated and not used for qualifying higher education expense. In these cases, the rollover will generate an income tax even though no money has been withdrawn from the portfolio. Some states also impose a penalty tax on withdrawals from the 529 Plan account within a stipulated period of time (typically ranging from one to three years).

Another recent change is the recapture of state income tax deductions when you roll out of a plan that you received an income tax deduction for when you first contributed to the account. A number of states have passed laws allowing for the recapture of income tax benefits when consumers move their 529 plan accounts out of their home state. This only occurs when a tax deduction was allowed at the time of contribution.

Most states afford an income tax break at the time of withdrawal. There are a few states that tax both residents and nonresidents, and these states' plans must be reviewed carefully to determine whether the income tax at the state level will cause an unnecessary drain on the College Savings Plan proceeds. (Consult a tax professional before making any investment decisions.)

Another word of caution—some of these states allow for both the state's residents and nonresidents to be tax-free due to the state's conformity with federal law.

There is a concern that the states that have adopted federal law—without their own state exemption for residents—may see the federal law sunset at the end of 2010.

What all of this should highlight is that not all College Savings Plans are the same. In selecting an appropriate plan for your family, thought must be given to issues of taxation—more specifically, to issues of state income taxes. Many investors and advisors will focus on the risk tolerance and state tax deductibility of contributions, but the analysis should also include an understanding of the state taxation of *withdrawals* from the College Savings Plan.

4

BENEFICIARY PLANNING

One of the most flexible components of the College Savings Plan is the ability to change the beneficiary of an account from time to time. The following material outlines the basic components to selecting and maintaining a beneficiary of a 529 College Savings Plan, as well as some creative planning opportunities.

The Basics

Internal Revenue Code Section 529 allows for the establishment of a College Savings Account for the purpose of meeting the qualified higher education expenses of the designated beneficiary of the account. Code Section 529, in part, provides that a *designated beneficiary* means:

(A) the individual designated at the commencement of participation in the qualified tuition program as the beneficiary of amounts paid (or to be paid) to the program,

(B) in the case of a change in beneficiaries...the individual who is the new beneficiary....

This means that any person may be a beneficiary of a College Savings Account. The individual does not need to be a child, a relative, or have any other traditional connection to the account owner. In fact, under many states' plans, it is permissible to name a spouse or the account owner's self as the beneficiary of the account.

The College Savings Plan also allows for the change of beneficiary on an account at anytime. It allows the changes to be free of any taxation or penalty provided certain rules regarding *family members* are followed.

One great uncertainty facing each person saving for a child's college expenses is the question of *what to do if the child does not attend college*? The College Savings Plan affords the flexibility to redirect assets to another child or relative that will be attending college. This ability to change the beneficiary of an account is a key component of the College Savings Plan.

If the savings account is in the form of a traditional taxable savings account, then the owner of the account can simply save the money for some other need. If the account was established in the form of a custodial (UGMA/UTMA) account, then regardless of whether the child attends college, the assets in the account belong to the child. The inability to change the beneficiary of a custodial account is perhaps the greatest negative to opening such an account.

A true advantage of the College Savings Account compared with other types of savings vehicles for college can be seen when undertaking financial planning with young families. Consider the young married couple planning on having children in the next several years. Basic financial planning tells us that the sooner assets are invested on a tax-deferred basis, the greater the potential growth opportunity. Under the *old* UGMA/UTMA approach to saving for college, no account could be established until a child was born.

With the College Savings Account, this young couple can establish several College Savings Accounts, naming each other (or themselves) as beneficiaries, and begin the tax-deferred savings. The beneficiary of the account can be changed to name a newborn child at some point down the road. This is the first time that a tax-deferred investment account for a child not yet born can be established. Once again, there may be a substantial difference achieved merely by starting sooner.

Changing the Beneficiary

The single most frequently asked question—*what if my child does not go to college?*—leads to one of the greatest elements of the Section 529 College Savings Plan. The College Savings Plan allows for virtually complete control by the owner over who will benefit from the College Savings Account, and when. Again, allowing the owner of the account the ability to change beneficiaries of the account at anytime affords the College Savings Plan one of its greatest advantages over other forms of saving for college.

One interesting detail about establishing a College Savings Account is that you do not need to tell the beneficiary that you have established the account for him or her. This allows for complete privacy in the matter of selecting and possibly changing your desired beneficiary. For many reasons, including a child who does not end up attending college, the owner of the account may wish to change the beneficiary of the account from time to time.

The rules allow for the owner of the account to change the beneficiary at any time he or she wants.

How to Change the Beneficiary

Changing the beneficiary on a College Savings Account is extremely easy. The Plan Managers all have a standard Beneficiary Change Form that can be used to revise a beneficiary designation. Completing the form and filing it with the Plan Manager is all that is required. As with all beneficiary designations, it makes good sense to keep a copy of what you filed. It is also sensible to ask the Plan Manager to send you a copy of the beneficiary designation at least once a year to confirm that the Plan Manager has the correct information.

Frequency of Changing the Beneficiary

The rules allow you to change the beneficiary of the College Savings Account any time you like. The problem is that you may cause the account to be taxed—or in some cases, taxed and penalized—if you change the beneficiary to a person who does not qualify for tax-free beneficiary changes. To qualify for a tax-free, penalty-free change of beneficiary of an account, the new beneficiary must fall into a *member of the family* class of individuals of the old beneficiary.

Tax-Free Beneficiary Changes

Recent tax law changes expanded the definition of *member of the family* so that many individuals qualify for tax-free, penalty-free change in beneficiary. Remember, when trying to determine whether a new beneficiary falls within one of the relationships, you must measure from the *old beneficiary*, not the account owner. This means if a child is named as the original beneficiary of a College Savings Plan and the parent decides to make a change to the beneficiary, then the new beneficiary must be a relation of the child (the old beneficiary).

EXAMPLE

Sam sets up a College Savings Account for his best friend's daughter, Kim. Kim decides not to go to college and starts a family of her own. Sam can change the beneficiary to Kim's child, tax-free.

The following is a list of relations according to the definition of a member of the family:

- son or daughter, or a descendant of either;
- stepson or stepdaughter;
- brother, sister, stepbrother, or stepsister;
- father or mother, or ancestor of either;
- stepfather or stepmother;
- son or daughter of a brother or sister (nephews/nieces);
- brother or sister of a mother or father (uncle/aunt);
- son-in-law or daughter-in-law;
- mother-in-law or father-in-law;
- brother-in-law or sister-in-law;
- spouse of the beneficiary of any of the above; or,
- the beneficiary's first cousin.

EXAMPLE

Cathy established a College Savings Account for the benefit of her son, Rob, age 15. At age 18, Rob decides to travel the world rather than attend college. Cathy obtains a change of beneficiary designation form from the Plan Manager and names her daughter, Michelle (age 13) as the new College Savings Plan beneficiary. This qualifies as a tax-free change of beneficiary, since Michelle is a *member of the family* in relation to Rob.

Cathy could also name a nephew or niece as beneficiary if she chose to, and it would also qualify as a tax-free change of beneficiary.

If Cathy, as the account owner, names a person who is not related to Rob (the original beneficiary), the change in beneficiary would not be tax-free. If she named the son of her next door neighbor as beneficiary, such a change would force the College Savings Plan to be taxed and, as the account owner, Cathy would also have to pay a penalty tax of 10% of the income of the account.

Maximum Contribution Limits and Changes to Existing Plans

It is important to remember when changing a beneficiary on a College Savings Account that the total amount set aside for that beneficiary cannot exceed the *maximum contribution limit* for that beneficiary. As you may recall, each state establishes the maximum amount that may be set aside for a child's higher education expenses. Exceeding this limit may result in an unnecessary income tax and penalty. The Plan Manager will have a procedure to alert you to any excess contribution.

In addition, most Plan Managers will ask that you sign a statement that the total of all College Savings Accounts for the beneficiary do not exceed the maximum contribution limit. It is important to be certain you know the limits in your state to avoid any surprises.

EXAMPLE

Dianne established a College Savings Account for the benefit of her son, Jim, age 15. At age 18, Jim decides to travel the world rather than attend college. Dianne obtains a change of beneficiary designation form from the Plan Manager and names her daughter, Alexia (age 13), as the new College Savings Plan beneficiary. The account at that time has a total value of $200,000.

On the date that Dianne names Alexia as the beneficiary of the account, Alexia had a separate College Savings Account with a total of $75,000 of asset value. The state in which Dianne resides has established a maximum contribution limit of $232,000 for the year in which the beneficiary change was to be made.

This change of beneficiary designation to Alexia exceeds the maximum contribution limit by $43,000 ($200,000 + $75,000 = $275,000 and $275,000 - $232,000 = $43,000). The Plan Manager will have to refuse the excess contribution. If the Plan Manager did not refuse the addition, the change of beneficiary would not qualify in total as a tax-free change, and would subject the excess contributions ($43,000) to tax and penalty.

Tax-Free Changes

Section 529 allows for tax-free changes to your College Savings Plan if one of the following happens within sixty days of any of the listed changes.

1. *Change of Plan Manager for the benefit of the same beneficiary (rollovers).* The rules allow you to change from one Plan Manager to another, provided that the account opened with the new Plan Manager is for the same designated beneficiary. This change of Plan Managers, perhaps in an effort to secure better investment performance or to secure a state income tax deduction for contributions, requires that this change occur only once per year. Any change of Plan Manager more often than once per year will cause the entire account to be taxed to the owner, who will also incur the 10% penalty for failing to adhere to the rules of the College Savings Plan.

   A recent development with respect to state income taxes on 529 Plans relates to *rollovers* from one state's plan to another. Under Section 529, you are permitted to roll over plan assets for the same beneficiary from one state's 529 Plan to another one time per twelve-month period. Even though federal law allows this to be a federal income tax-free event, many states are now beginning to tax participants on rollovers as though the assets in the 529 Plan were liquidated and not used for qualifying higher education expense. In these cases, the rollover will generate an income tax even though no money has been withdrawn from the portfolio. Some states also impose a penalty tax on withdrawals from the 529 Plan account within a stipulated period of time (typically ranging from one to three years).

Another recent change is the recapture of the state income tax deduction when you roll out of a plan that you received an income tax deduction for when you first contributed to the account. A number of states have passed laws allowing for the recapture of income tax benefits when consumers move their 529 Plan accounts out of their home state. This only occurs when a tax deduction was allowed at the time of contribution.

2. *Change of account in the same program.* You can change accounts within the same Plan Manager's plan, provided the beneficiary is *not* the same beneficiary for whom the plan was originally established. For this change to be considered tax-free, the *member of the family* rules must be followed.

3. *Change to a different program.* You can change to a different Plan Manager's plan, provided the beneficiary is *not* the same beneficiary for whom the plan was originally established. For this change to be considered tax-free, the *member of the family* rules must be followed.

Financial Aid

As a general rule, federal financial aid for college is calculated by factoring the income and assets of both the parents and the students. This is done by the Department of Education on its commonly used form, the *Free Application for Federal Student Aid* (FAFSA). The formulas typically provide that 50% of a student's income and 35% of the student's assets are treated as available to be used for college expenses. The rules also provide that, subject to certain allowances and expenses, between 20% and 50% of a parent's income and approximately 6% of a parent's assets are treated as available for college expense. For this reason, a 529 College Savings Plan account should not be owned by a child, since a greater portion of the account would be treated as available for college expense.

Perhaps this leads to a planning opportunity. An approach that might be taken is to have the College Savings Account owned by someone other than a parent—perhaps an aunt, uncle, or grandparent. In such a case, the College Savings Account would not be included in the family's financial aid picture because the parents and children do not own the account. Of course, such a strategy has many pitfalls, including the risk that the owner dies, the owner files for bankruptcy or divorce, or the owner changes the beneficiary to be someone other than the child for whom it was originally intended. Nonetheless, under certain family circumstances, this may well work.

5

OWNERSHIP AND MAINTENANCE

Each 529 College Savings Plan must have an *owner* designated for the account. The owner will be the person who has control over decisions like who the beneficiary will be, when the money will be withdrawn and for whom, and how the investments of the College Savings Plan will be maintained. Often, this will be the person who opens the account. For varying reasons, including financial aid and estate planning concerns, ownership of a College Savings Plan may be in the hands of a trust, a grandparent, or another family member. When establishing the College Savings Plan account, the Plan Manager will have the owner designated on the account opening form.

Lifetime Issues

While it is clear that the owner can change the beneficiary at any time (hopefully as a tax-free change to a *member of the family*), changing ownership does not appear to be as easy. Most plans are silent on the issue, but it is reasonable to assume that changing ownership is problematic. What is clear is that the transfer of ownership, if possible under a particular state's plan, will incur a federal (and possibly a state) gift tax.

Transfer at Death

Each Plan Manager will establish their own detailed rules as to what steps are to be taken should the account owner die. However, you can generally expect the steps discussed in this section to occur in most states.

Successor Owner Named

In most cases when an account is opened, the forms provided by the Plan Manager will allow an account owner to list a *successor owner* (next owner) in the event the original owner should pass away. It is important that these forms be properly completed to prevent unintended consequences if the account owner passes away. It is important to periodically review the forms completed when the account was opened. Be certain there is a proper beneficiary named and there is a successor owner named in the event the owner should pass away.

No Successor Owner Named

When an owner of a College Savings Account dies without having named a successor owner, many Plan Manager participation agreements will have a default owner or will look to the *probate* or *surrogate* law of the state in which the owner lived. (This is the state law that controls what happens to assets when someone passes away.) In essence, the owner's *last will and testament* will dictate who is to become the new owner of the account. This may prove to be a serious issue, as many states have probate laws that divide assets into equal or unequal shares for various beneficiaries.

Some states may provide that upon someone's death (assuming they died without a will), the spouse is to inherit one-half of the assets (which would include the College Savings Plan asset), and the children are to inherit the other one-half. In such a case, the College Savings Plan account may actually have two, three, or more owners.

EXAMPLE

Shelia established a College Savings Account for the benefit of her son, with Shelia named as the owner of the account. Several years later, Shelia dies. She does not have a will and is survived by her husband and two children. Under the laws of the state in which Shelia resided, a person who dies without having a will has their assets divided so that one-half goes to the spouse, with the balance being equally divided between the children. The result is that the College Savings Account will be owned one-half by her husband and one-quarter by each of the two children.

Consider this problem: a person who is single has a College Savings Account for a nephew, and dies without a will. If the owner had no parents but three siblings, the state's laws might have all three siblings inherit the account. In this case, two of the siblings who do not have children might want to distribute their share of the College Savings Account, leaving only the one sibling with a child to keep the account intact.

To avoid these problems, be certain a contingent or successor owner is named on the College Savings

Account, or that the terms of your will make a specific reference as to who will become the new owner of the College Savings Account if you were to pass away.

Trusts as Owners

For hundreds of years, trusts—whether revocable or irrevocable—have served as owners of assets as a means to perpetuate control over the assets. Some families may wish to consider the use of a trust as the owner or as successor owner of a College Savings Account to be certain there is continuity of control over the assets in it. This may be particularly helpful in the context of establishing a College Savings Account for the benefit of grandchildren or even great-grandchildren.

Furthermore, using a trust instrument as a successor owner may allow the account owner greater control over the eventual destiny of the College Savings Plan assets than he or she might have otherwise had.

Investment Options

One feature of a 529 College Savings Plan is that the owner of the account is not allowed direct control over the investments of the 529 Plan account. The consumer is limited to designating the appropriate style or investment option that he or she desires. At one time, each of the Plan Managers offered only a few different investment options for the consumer. Over the past several years, the offerings by the various 529 Plan Managers have increased substantially. This section describes the most traditional investment options offered to the consumer.

Age-Based Portfolios

An *age-based portfolio* is designed to take into account a beneficiary's age when constructing the portfolio. Many of the Plan Managers have portfolios constructed based upon the year in which the child will attend college. A common feature of these portfolios is that the allocation of assets between stocks and bonds in a portfolio adjusts as the child grows older. Generally, the younger the beneficiary, the greater the percentage of a portfolio that will contain stocks. As the child approaches college age, the portfolio is gradually shifted so a larger portion of the portfolio is made up of bonds for the years just prior to attending college.

Many of these age-based portfolios offer a selection of the risk the account owner is willing to take. Often, these portfolios will provide the option of selecting a conservative age-based portfolio, a moderate risk age-based portfolio, or an aggressive age-based portfolio.

Static Portfolios

Many of the 529 College Savings Plan Managers offer a *static* or *custom* type of portfolio for account owners who want to invest the plan assets without basing the investments on the age of the beneficiary. While the age-based portfolio is changed over time, the static portfolio will remain constant regardless of the beneficiary's age. These types of portfolios are created with certain amounts of stocks, bonds, and cash to suit the account owners *risk tolerance*. The selection made by the account owner as to the nature of the investment (aggressive growth, growth, etc.) will remain as the investment policy for the 529 Plan investments until a change is made to the selected investment strategy.

Many 529 Plans are managed by mutual fund companies who will construct the age-based and static portfolios by using combinations of their existing mutual fund investments. The astute investor will want to understand all of the underlying mutual fund investments, as well as any fees and expenses associated with them.

Principal-Protected Portfolios

Recently, many 529 Plan Managers have been offering a form of *principal-protected investment option*. This type of option guarantees that the contributions to the 529 Plan are protected from a loss in the marketplace due to fluctuations in the underlying investments. These investments are given some percentage of increase based upon an index used by the Plan Manager and are protected against loss in the portfolio.

Fees and Expenses

Every 529 College Savings Plan charges the account owner expenses for managing and administering the 529 College Savings Plan. These fees include services for managing the underlying investments, actual expenses of underlying mutual funds, administrative fees, management fees, and marketing services. The following are the most common fees and expenses.

1. *Account Maintenance Fee.* The account maintenance fee is a specific dollar amount charged to the account on a quarterly or annual basis as a fee to maintain the account.

2. *Asset-Based Management Fee.* This is the fee charged by the Plan Manager as compensation for creating and maintaining the investments of the 529 Plan

account. This fee, charged as a percentage, is multiplied by the amount in the account to determine the actual dollar cost. This fee is typically a combination of the state administration fee (sometimes known as state authority fee), a program manager fee, and an investment services fee.

3. *Underlying Fund Expenses.* Many 529 Plans charge a separate fee to the 529 Plan account for the actual mutual fund expenses incurred in the various portfolios. Some 529 Plans include this particular fee as part of the asset-based management fee.

4. *State Authority Fee.* This is the amount a state receives for its role in managing and administering the state's 529 Plan. The amount is often included in the asset-based management fee charged to the 529 Plan account.

Fee Structures

In addition to the administrative and management fees that account owners will incur, there are also *sales charges* and *sales loads* charged to the consumer at the time contributions are made to the account. Many states allow their residents to invest in the home state 529 Plan directly through the State Treasurer's office with little or no sales charge. However, there are generally several different fee structures available when a 529 Plan is obtained through a financial advisor.

1. *Fee Structure A/(A Shares).* The consumer will pay an initial sales load or charge as a percentage of the assets contributed to the 529 Plan.

2. *Fee Structure B/(B Shares).* No initial sales load is charged, but a deferred sales load/charge is incurred if withdrawals or rollovers occur within a specified number of years. This is typically done on a sliding scale, with the highest percentage charged for withdrawals during the earlier years and a smaller charge in the later years.

3. *Fee Structure C/(C Shares).* A deferred sales charge is incurred if distributions or rollovers occur within one year of contribution. Otherwise, the only charge is an annual administration fee that is higher than the administration fees incurred under shares A or B.

6

THE ROLE OF THE ADVISOR

As they now exist, College Savings Plans come in two basic types. There are plans you can obtain without advice (*retail plans*) and plans you obtain through an advisor (*advisor plans*). An example of a retail plan is *Fidelity Retail* or the plans offered by the *Teachers Insurance Annuity Association* (TIAA/CREF). An advisor plan would be a plan such as *Merrill Lynch's Next Gen Plan* or the *Fidelity Advisor Plan*. Your choice then is to purchase a College Savings Plan directly from the Plan Manager (the retail plan) or purchase the plan from an advisor (the advisor plan). Some states also allow its residents to invest in the plan directly with the State Treasurer's office (a version of the retail plan).

The key difference between the two types of plans is the advice component that the advisor plans have. How important is advice? In this era, it seems to be wise to have a professional financial advisor sitting at the table when important financial decisions are made.

Issues for the Advisor

While the College Savings Plan mandates that the consumer not have direct control over the investment of plan assets, the consumer still has substantial input into exactly how the savings plan will work. While fees may be involved, an advisor might be best suited to assist the consumer with the following issues.

1. *Tax Issues.* Each College Savings Plan, as administered by the state of creation, has its own rules about state tax deductibility of investments and state taxation of distributions. An advisor should be in a position to analyze the various state tax issues and quantify any possible state tax benefits available.

2. *Investment Issues.* Plan Managers have responded to the consumer's request for greater investment options and have developed many different investment options for the assets in a College Savings Plan. Day after day, Plan Managers add new offerings within their College Savings Plans. In many cases available investment options are provided by many of the traditional investment and mutual fund companies well-known across America. A sample of available investment options include:

   - age-based portfolio;
   - balanced portfolio;
   - growth;
   - aggressive growth;
   - US Large Capitalization equity growth;
   - US Small Capitalization equity growth;
   - US Blended Capitalization;
   - high-yield bond fund;
   - capital preservation;
   - international equity—large and small capitalization; and,
   - investment grade bond funds.

The professional investment advisor is well-suited to assist a family in selecting the best investment strategy for the College Savings Plan. The professional advisor may also be called upon to analyze for an investor the new fund offerings being brought to market on almost a daily basis by Plan Managers. As the Plan Managers compete for available 529 Plan investors, one approach will be for Plan Managers to differentiate themselves by the quantity (and hopefully, quality) of the investment options available.

3. *Performance Issues.* The College Savings Plan is new to the investment world, and for this reason, analyzing returns on investment for a particular portfolio must be viewed in the short-term. As the Plan Managers gain experience and historical data, the performance of one Plan Manager's fund when compared to another Plan Manager's fund will become a key factor in determining the most appropriate Plan Manager and investments for the particular College Savings Account. Investors will be in a position to analyze one Plan Manager's performance for a particular fund versus another. The professional advisor is perhaps best suited for this type of analysis.

EXAMPLE

Kelly opens a College Savings Account and will receive a $400 savings on her state personal income tax return for contributions made to the plan. She chose an age-based program to invest in. While on its face this seems

continued...

appropriate, perhaps a different course of action would be taken if she knew that the age-based program managed by her state's Plan Manager was under-performing all other Plan Managers by a substantial amount. In such a case, she might opt to forgo the $400 in tax savings to achieve a better return from a Plan Manager who was experiencing a better investment return.

4. *Implementation and Monitoring of Plan.* The professional advisor is uniquely qualified to assist the investor in establishing the College Savings Plan and monitoring the plan over time. The professional advisor can assist in a number of issues that require constant monitoring of a College Savings Plan, including:

- proper ownership of the plan;
- successor ownership should the plan owner die;
- beneficiary planning and changing of beneficiaries;
- plan performance and investment return; and,
- monitoring changes in the plan itself—increase in funding limits and expansion of options.

5. *Legislative Changes.* An advisor can also keep an investor up-to-date with the latest information about plan changes and legislative changes that affect the plan. As Plan Managers change their plans and states change the rules governing the plans, it is crucial to stay current.

7

ESTATE PLANNING AND THE COLLEGE SAVINGS PLAN

Much of our focus has been on the opportunity the College Savings Plan provides in the context of saving for college. Not quite as obvious is the estate planning opportunity to be achieved by using the College Savings Plan as a wealth-transfer vehicle.

Federal Estate Planning Basics

The College Savings Plan is a federal program administered by each state in a slightly different manner. Since each state will have a different way of dealing with gift and estate taxes, discussion here will focus solely on the federal estate tax and gift tax systems. As with the income tax differences from state to state, which make the selection of an appropriate College Savings Account a complicated task, the state gift and estate taxes must be considered.

Under the current federal system governing gifts and estate taxes, everyone is allowed to make gifts each year to as many people (related or not) as they like in an amount up to $11,000 to each—free of any gift tax. Married couples can join together to double this per person gift to an annual $22,000. In addition to these gifts, each person has a lifetime $1,000,000 exemption amount for gifts above this annual limit. To the extent the lifetime exemption amount is not used, then the remaining balance can be used at death to offset any estate taxes. This exemption amount is scheduled to increase substantially over the next several years.

EXAMPLE

Jill would like to make a gift of $11,000 to each of her three children. This gift qualifies under the allowable gift tax annual exclusion, and is a nontaxable gift that does not require the filing of a gift tax return.

If she and her husband, Bill, want to make a joint gift, a check in the amount of $22,000 to each child would still qualify the gift under the allowable gift tax annual exclusion as a nontaxable gift. Since they are joining together to treat the gifts as being half from each person (*gift-splitting*), there is still no gift tax to be paid. However, they do need to file a gift tax return to document the gift-splitting.

EXAMPLE

Carrie has three children. She would like to make a gift to each of her three children. She writes a check to each child in the amount of $111,000. The first $11,000 of each gift is a nontaxable gift under the gift tax annual exclusion. The additional $100,000 per child amount in excess of the $11,000 reduces Carrie's lifetime

continued...

exemption amount from the original $1,000,000 by the amount of these gifts ($300,000). She must file a gift tax return to report that she has used up a portion of her lifetime exemption amount, but no gift tax is paid.

Gift Rules

In an effort to help families begin the savings process, the Section 529 rules allow for the *front-end loading* of a College Savings Account. This means that the rules allow for more than the annual $11,000 per person gift. The rules allow for five times that amount. (It is recognized as $11,000 each year over five years that are allowed by the rules.) A single person can transfer $55,000 to a College Savings Account for a person and not have any amount of the gift reduce his or her lifetime credit amount. Married couples can join together to make this a $110,000 gift without any reducing their lifetime credits. By setting up the gift-giving rules this way, the tax-deferred savings is more meaningful.

The rules even allow you to stay up-to-date with current gift-giving law. The rules provide that if the amount of the annual exclusion increases and you have already made a gift that you are *stretching* over the five-year allowable period, then you are allowed to add to the account in an amount designed to let you use the full annual gift exclusion amount.

EXAMPLE

In 2000 (when $10,000 was the maximum tax-free gift allowed), Amy made a gift of $50,000 to her daughter and had the money invested in a College

continued...

Savings Account. Amy made the necessary election to have the amounts spread evenly over five years, so that the gift is treated as the allowable $10,000 per year. In 2002, the tax law changed and the annual exclusion amount increased to $11,000 per year per person. Amy is allowed to add to the College Savings Account the increase of $1,000 per year for each of the remaining years the original gift is being spread. In this case, Amy may add up to $3,000 for years 2002, 2003, and 2004.

There is a catch when making these larger up-front gifts. If you make a gift that is more than the annual amount (currently $11,000), the rules give you the option of either treating the excess as being used up equally over a five-year period as though you annually made the $11,000 gift or using up some of your lifetime $1,000,000 exemption amount. Since most people attempt to save the exemption amount, or certainly use the *free* annual exclusion amount first, it will be common for people to use the ability to *spread* the gifts over five years. If you do this, and you pass away during this five-year period, part of the original gift (not the growth) will be brought back into your estate for tax purposes.

EXAMPLE

In 2002, Claire made a gift of $55,000 to her daughter and has the money invested in a College Savings Account. She made the necessary election to have the amounts in excess of the annual $11,000 amount (here, an excess of $44,000) spread evenly over the
continued...

remaining four years. Claire died in 2004, when the College Savings Account value $75,000. Her estate must include the portion of the original gift that has not been fully covered by the five annual exclusions.

In this case, Mary will have used three exclusions (2002, 2003, and 2004 at $11,000 each year) and will have two remaining years of exclusions that have not been used. For this reason, Claire's estate (for tax purposes) must include the $22,000 (2005 and 2006 at $11,000 each year) of gifts that were not covered by the exclusion. Even though $22,000 worth of the gift is being included in Claire's taxable estate, the growth that has been achieved on this money does not get included.

Control

One of the more amazing things about the College Savings Plan (and the related gift planning) is that this may be the first gift ever to be created in which the person giving the gift can redirect who will receive the gift. Under traditional gift tax rules, if a person made a gift but kept some element of control over both the gift and who the eventual beneficiary would be (or just had the power to change beneficiaries even if the power was never exercised), the gift would be treated as an *incomplete gift*. This means that the full amount of the original gift and any *appreciation* on the gift would not be treated as a gift for gift tax purposes. When the person who made the original gift, but kept control, eventually died, his or her estate would be taxed in full for the value of the gift.

The 529 Plan rules specifically allow for the owner of the account (most often the person who puts the money into the account) to maintain control over the account—

even control over who will receive it and when. The rules specifically state that retaining this control will not cause the amount in the account to be taxed to the owner at his or her death. Finally, people can make gifts but feel as though they did not give up that single most important item—control.

EXAMPLE

Cynthia makes a gift of $11,000 and places the money in a College Savings Account. Cynthia names her daughter, Ellen, as the beneficiary. Ten years later, when the account has grown to be $60,000, Cynthia takes Ellen's name off the account and places Steven's name on the account. Even though Cynthia has made a gift, she has kept control over who will have the beneficial enjoyment. At Cynthia's death, no amount of the gift will be included in her taxable estate for estate tax purposes.

Even beyond the ability to change the beneficiary, the owner of the account has the ability to close the account and take back all of the money at anytime. Of course, doing so will subject the assets to the ordinary income tax on all of the gains, as well as the penalty tax of 10%. In some cases, this may seem a small price to pay to be certain the *right* thing happens.

Creative Estate Planning

Never before have estate planners had such a powerful gift-giving tool to add to their arsenal of gift-giving strategies. The ability to grow assets tax-deferred, while continuing to maintain complete control over who is the beneficiary, affords families with estate tax exposure a new way to plan away these estate taxes.

For a family that has a substantial net worth that will cause them to face an estate tax, the funding of a College Savings Account is not just to save for college. It is also an opportunity to save for college for grandchildren and great-grandchildren—even those not yet born. Since the College Savings Account allows for the changing of beneficiary—tax-free at any time—the opportunity exists to begin shifting assets to a lower generation without really knowing who will eventually benefit from the gift. By using the College Savings Plan as a gift-giving tool, it is now possible to make gifts and begin the shifting of all growth on those gifts, without using any lifetime gift tax exemption amount, and never losing control. (We recommend the reader consult an attorney for specific estate planning assistance.)

EXAMPLE

Georgia makes a gift of $11,000 into a College Savings Account and names herself as beneficiary. Georgia does this each year for a series of five years. Twenty years later, when the account has grown to a value of $200,000, Georgia takes her name off the account and names her fifteen-year-old grandson as the beneficiary. During all of the years prior to naming her grandson, and the years after naming him, Georgia has maintained control over the account, including when it would be used and for whom. It is important to note that the naming of the grandson to be the beneficiary of the College Savings Account may incur both a gift tax and a generation

continued...

skipping tax. No income tax would be incurred as the naming of a grandchild falls within the *member of the family* rules.

The Double-Dip Opportunity

Current gift-giving rules allow for the payment of tuition expenses without having to use any of your annual gift-giving exclusion amounts or the lifetime exemption amount. For this reason, grandparents are often advised to write a check directly to pay tuition at a school their grandchild attends rather than making the gift to the grandchild to use for tuition. In fact, there are cases where older individuals are encouraged to prepay all four years of college tuition for their grandchildren in an effort to use as much of their assets as possible. That way, those assets will not be included in their taxable estates. When someone is older and may not survive all four years of college tuition-paying, the prepayment option makes sense.

In the context of the College Savings Account, this type of planning continues to make sense. If a grandparent is in a position to pay the tuition directly to the college or university, then he or she should do so. In doing so, the amounts transferred to the school will escape all forms of gift tax and estate tax under existing law. Once the tuition has been paid, the grandparent can then add additional gift funds to a College Savings Account to be used to pay room and board, books, supplies, etc.

> **EXAMPLE**
>
> Virginia writes a check of $30,000 to Yale University for her granddaughter's college tuition. In addition, Virginia makes a gift of $11,000 to her granddaughter and places the money in a College Savings Account to be used to pay for books, supplies, equipment, etc. All of this $41,000 is tax-free.

The Unintended Gift Tax Consequence

The owner of the College Savings Account can change the beneficiary at anytime as long as the *member of the family* sets of rules are followed. However, when a change of beneficiary moves the beneficiary to someone a generation lower than the original beneficiary, then a gift has been made. In this case, the gift is treated as being made by the beneficiary to the new beneficiary. If the new beneficiary is more than one generation below the original beneficiary, then not only is it a gift, but it may also be a *generation-skipping gift* and may subject the assets to the *generation-skipping tax*. This is potentially dangerous, as the original beneficiary has no control over the change of beneficiary, but is responsible for the gift tax. This is a technical issue that Congress needs to address.

> **EXAMPLE**
>
> In 2000, Valerie made a gift of $55,000 to her daughter, Kim, and had the money invested in a College Savings Account. Fifteen years later, when the account
>
> *continued...*

value has grown to $150,000, Valerie removes her daughter's name and places her granddaughter's name on the College Savings Account. In this case, the naming of the granddaughter is treated as a gift from Kim to the granddaughter of the entire amount value of the College Savings Account. Kim would use her annual gift tax exclusion amount, as well as some amount of her lifetime credit exemption amount, to prevent this gift from resulting in a gift tax.

Post-Death Trust Issues

Of great concern are the steps that need to be taken when the owner of a College Savings Account dies, leaving a will that transfers all assets to a trust. Sometimes trusts that receive assets at death are extremely complicated and may not be an appropriate place for a College Savings Account. In fact, it is common for married couples to have special types of wills and trusts designed to utilize the federal unified credit against estate taxes. These types of trusts, known as *bypass* trusts, mandate certain uses and distributions of principal and income. If the College Savings Account is an asset that gets swept into a bypass trust, unfortunate and unintended results may occur.

If the bypass trust is drafted in a traditional manner, allowing for the use of the assets for a variety of needs (including education expenses), then the College Savings Account may continue to work as originally intended.

A further problem that may occur after death is when a College Savings Account is transferred into a marital trust. One form of a marital trust, known as a *Qualified Terminable Interest Property Trust* (QTIP) is generally for the surviving spouse only. A QTIP trust is required by tax law to generate income on the principal to the trust. This is far different from the College Savings Account, which does not generally create income, and if it did, would not have any income distributed. The trustee of a QTIP trust might be put in a position of having to close the College Savings Account and withdraw the money as cash to properly move forward in his or her job as trustee.

In either case, if the College Savings Account was intact at the time of the spouse's death, and the account was in a QTIP trust, the entire account balance would be included in the surviving spouse's estate under the federal estate tax rules applicable to QTIP trusts. The solution is to properly plan for a successor or contingent owner on the College Savings Account to be certain the ownership of the account does not end up in an unfortunate trust setting.

Death of a Beneficiary

The law provides that if a beneficiary of a College Savings Plan dies, then the full value of the College Savings Account is included in the beneficiary's estate for estate tax purposes. It would be unusual for a child for whom a College Savings Account had been established to pass away. However, there are times when an account owner will know of the possible impending death of the beneficiary. The owner would then change the beneficiary to prevent any amount from being included in the beneficiary's estate.

As noted, the first one million dollars of assets in an estate pass free of federal estate tax. Therefore, the inclusion in a beneficiary's estate is only an estate tax issue when the beneficiary has one million dollars or more of assets, plus a College Savings Account when he or she dies. The *Economic Growth and Tax Relief Reconciliation Act of 2001* repeals the estate tax for one year in 2010. Without further action by Congress, the 2001 federal estate tax rules will be reinstated in 2011, with a $1 million exemption equivalent.

EXAMPLE

In 2004, Jane, a beneficiary of a 529 Plan account, passed away. At the time of her death, she was unmarried and had total assets of $1,600,000. In addition, Jane was the beneficiary of a College Savings Account that had $200,000. The combined amount of $1,800,000 is more than the existing estate tax-free credit of $1,500,000. For this reason, Jane's estate will pay estate tax on the amount greater than $1,500,000 ($300,000).

Strange Possibilities

Congress will need to continually update and modify the Section 529 rules. As presently drafted, unintended results may occur from time to time.

Consider the circumstance in which a father makes annual gifts to his children's several College Savings Accounts in annual amounts of $44,000 ($11,000 for each of his four children). The father dies and provides for no successor owner in the Plan Managers records. In such a case, the father's will takes control, and if the father's will leaves everything to his wife, she becomes the new owner of the accounts.

Under the estate tax rules, nothing is included in the father's estate, as these were completed gifts utilizing the father's annual exclusions. Even though the father utilized his annual gift tax exclusion, the ownership of the account passes to his wife, not to the beneficiaries. The wife could now close the 529 accounts and take back all the money in the accounts.

To prevent any problems, it is important to have an updated set of ownership forms on these documents. In addition, it may make sense to begin having wills specifically state that a College Savings Plan owned by a person who passes away is to pass to a specific individual who will be the new owner of the account.

What happens if one of the children for whom an account was established were to pass away? Under the general rules, the child would include in his or her own estate the full amount of the account. This full inclusion occurs even though the mother continues to maintain complete control over the account and can name a new beneficiary or even distribute the account for herself. It is strange that the beneficiary is subjected to estate taxation on assets in an account that he or she did not have control of, and might never have benefited from (if the mother or father had changed the beneficiary to be someone else).

8

THE FUTURE OF 529 PLANS

Research indicates that College Savings Plans will be the single most popular investment vehicle over the next decade, with estimates of approximately $300 billion in 529 Plan assests expected before the end of thc decade. The ability to invest assets on a tax-deferred basis, remove the assets tax-free, and maintain complete control over the eventual destiny of the account assets makes the College Savings Plan an extraordinary opportunity.

Rebate Programs

As the College Savings Plan industry grows, new and interesting approaches to this field will take place. Some are already in progress. Two of the more creative businesses in this field can be found in *Upromise* and *BabyMint*. Both of these programs are designed to utilize corporate contributions to College Savings Plans on behalf of consumers purchasing the corporation's products. Much like earning free air miles by using an airline sponsored credit card, *Upromise* and *BabyMint* have affiliated themselves with a wide range of corporations that offer free rebate money into a consumer's

College Savings Plan. Each company has also affiliated with a credit card issuer, which allows members to earn 1% rebates on their purchases.

The *Upromise* website (**www.Upromise.com**) and the *BabyMint* website (**www.babymint.com**) provide a glimpse into the broad number of corporations offering free contributions to a College Savings Account when purchasing their goods. *Upromise's* partners include *ExxonMobil, AT&T, McDonald's, Staples*, 50,000 realtors, 7,000 restaurants, 16,000 grocery stores, over 100 online shops, and over 8,500 retail stores.

To obtain the *free* contribution, a consumer logs onto the *Upromise* website and registers one or more credit cards with *Upromise*. Once registered, any time a consumer purchases a product with one of the participating businesses using the registered credit card, a contribution is made to a College Savings Account for the consumer's child or family member.

BabyMint's business model is slightly different in that *BabyMint* utilizes gift certificates and online purchases with affiliated corporations to generate the contributions to a College Savings Account.

Regardless of where the contributions are deposited, in essence, free money is being contributed to an account for the benefit of someone's college education.

In recent months, several fund managers have begun adding credit card rebate programs to their offerings. Most notably is *Fidelity Investments*, who issue through MBNA a *Fidelity Rebate Card,* offering a 1% rebate into your Fidelity 529 Account for purchases with the credit card. School House Capital has a similar credit card offering, using the *BabyMint*-style approach of rebate dollars on credit cards, as well as additional rebates for purchases through their vendor network.

Affinity Programs

The future of College Savings Plans also lies with the *affinity* program. Programs such as the *Automobile Association of America* (AAA), *American Association of Retired Persons* (AARP), and medical and legal societies and associations, will begin to use the College Savings Plan as an added benefit for their membership. Much like the group provided life insurance, auto insurance, travel services, etc., the College Savings Plan will be added to the list of benefits available to association members. These types of College Savings Plans will be more in the nature of the corporate provided College Savings Plan. It is anticipated that these plans will be priced as an institutional product, affording the consumer the opportunity to obtain the College Savings Plan with the least amount of sales and related cost.

The challenge will be to create this opportunity in an environment focused first and foremost on advice and education. Given the broad choices within each different College Savings Plan and the tax, legal, beneficiary, and ownership issues to be grappled with, the *affinity group* provided College Savings Plan will need a strong advisory group in place to assist with advice and implementation issues.

GLOSSARY

A

account owner. The person who retains control over who the beneficiary will be and when withdrawals will be made from the College Savings Plan.

advisor plans. Plans that you can obtain through a professional advisor, unlike the retail plan.

age-based investment options. The portfolio is invested based upon the age of the child and the year he or she will be attending college. The longer the time in between now and the time he or she attends college, the more the investments will include stocks and equities. As the child ages and gets closer to the year of college, the investments are shifted more towards income investment and less towards stocks.

B

BabyMint. A program designed to use corporate contributions to College Savings Plans on behalf of consumers purchasing a particular corporation's products.

beneficiary. The person who will benefit from the College Savings Plan assets.

C

chase the best return. To try to time the best benefits of the market by jumping in and out of investments.

collateral. Money or property promised in order to get a loan and is used to pay back that loan should the debtor not pay.

College Savings Plan. A plan established and maintained by a state to assist families saving for college. These accounts are also known as Section 529 (of the Internal Revenue Code) plans and offer favorable tax benefits for using the plan to save money for college.

corporate-sponsored College Savings Plan. This is a College Savings Plan that is provided as a voluntary benefit to an employee by his or her employer.

Coverdell Education Savings Accounts. Often referred to as Education IRAs, these are savings/investment accounts into which a person can contribute a maximum of $2,000 per year.

Crummey Trust. A trust that allows for greater control over the principal of the trust for a longer priod of time. It allows the creator of the trust to stipulate at the time of creation how old a child must be to receive the trust principal.

custodial accounts. An account in which one person holds money or investments for the benefit of another person who is not yet of full age and legal capacity (*i.e.*, UGMA accounts and UTMA accounts).

D

disqualifying distribution. For 529 Plan purposes, removal of money from the 529 Account that is not used for qualified higher education expenses.

E

Economic Growth and Tax Relief Reconciliation Act of 2001 (EGTRRA). The law that ensures that no tax is paid on money that is withdrawn from a 529 Plan and used for qualified higher education expenses.

eligible education institution. Any accredited college, graduate school, or post secondary trade or vocational school that can participate in the federal student aid program.

estate taxes. Taxes charged by the IRS and some states on assets owned by a person at the time of their death.

F

front-end loading. Allowing for more than the annual $11,000 per person gift. A single person can transfer five times that amount at once ($55,000) to a College Savings Account for a person and not have any amount of the gift reduce their lifetime credit amount.

G

gift tax. A federal tax on the amount given as a gift that exceeds $11,000 per person per year, or $1,000,000 over the lifetime of the gift giver.

H

Hope Scholarship Credit. An income tax credit that has a maximum credit of $1,500 per student each calendar year.

I

institutional approach. To remove the management of investments from the individual to the professional.

irrevocable trusts. A trust (set of rules) that can never be changed once created.

K

kiddie tax. Rules that say that all income earned in accounts (such as custodial accounts) for a child under the age of 14 is taxable to the parent, at the parent's highest income tax bracket. Income earned in these types of accounts are fully taxable to the child, on the child's personal income tax return at the child's income tax rate, once the child is over the age of 14.

L

Lifetime Learning Credit. An income tax credit that has a maximum of $2,000 in calendar year 2004.

M

maximum contribution. A contribution that relates to the total amount that may be put aside in a College Savings Plan for one beneficiary.

P

penalty tax. For 529 Plan purposes, an amount equal to 10% of any money withdrawn from a 529 Account that is not used for qualified higher education expenses. This penalty is paid in addition to any regular income taxes on that withdrawal.

Plan Manager. A Plan Manager is the financial services company retained by a state to manage the state's College Savings 529 Plan.

Prepaid Tuition Plan. A state-sponsored plan that allows for the purchase of tuition credits for use at state participating colleges.

probate law. The laws of a particular state that determine where assets go at the time a person dies if the person did not have a will.

Q

qualified higher education expenses. A defined term relating to the expenses for which withdrawals from a College Savings Account are tax free. These include room, board, fees, books, supplies, etc.

Qualified Terminable Interest Property Trust (QTIP). One form of a marital trust, generally for the surviving spouse only, required by tax law to generate income on the principal to the trust.

R

refilling. The ability to add to an account's funds once a distribution has been made.

retail plans. 529 Plans that you can obtain without advice from a professional advisor.

risk-adjusted investments. Investments during a child's younger years that have a higher chance of loss than the investments during the years closer to the child attending college.

S

Section 2503(b) trust. A type of trust created by law, allowing for the saving of assets in an irrevocable trust, with all income earned being distributed to the child. The child pays all income tax on the earnings at the child's or parents' income tax rate, depending on the age of the child. When the child reaches age 25, the trustee must distribute the remaining trust assets outright to the child.

Section 2503(c) trust. A trust specially created by tax law, allowing for the saving of assets in an irrevocable trust, with all income earned being kept in the trust. The trust pays all income tax on the earnings at the trust's income tax rate.

Section 501(c)(3). The code section governing the characteristics to qualify an organization as a charity.

successor owner. The next owner of a given account.

sunset. Legislation coming to an end unless new legislation is passed to keep it alive.

T

tax deferral. Relates to the ability to invest assets and have all taxes on income and appreciation held off until sometime in the future.

tax deduction for contributions. This relates to the ability of a person to deduct on their tax return money they have invested on a College Savings Account.

U

Uniform Gift to Minors (UGMA). Under this Act, an adult holds assets for the benefit of a minor person.

Upromise. A program designed to use corporate contributions to College Savings Plans on behalf of consumers purchasing a particular corporation's products. Much like earning free air miles by using an airline sponsored credit card, *Upromise* has affiliated itself with a wide range of corporations that offer free rebate money into a consumer's College Savings Plan.

Uniform Transfers to Minors (UTMA). Under this Act, an adult holds assets for the benefit of a minor person.

APPENDIX: STATE PROGRAM INTERNET LINKS

The following are the World Wide Web addresses for the various College Savings Plans now available. You will see that some states have entered into agreements with more than one Plan Manager, so in these cases there is more than one plan available. Some states have not implemented their College Savings Plan as of the date of publication, and in those cases, no Web address is listed.

Alabama   Higher Education 529
                   www.treasury.state.al.us

Alaska   Manulife
                   www.manulifecollegesavings.com

                   T. Rowe Price
                   www.troweprice.com/collegesavings

                   U Alaska
                   www.uacollegesavings.com

Arizona   College Savings Bank
                   http://arizona.collegesavings.com

                   Pacific Funds 529
                   www.collegesavings.pacificlife.com

continued...

	Securities Mgmt & Research, Inc. www.smrinvest.com/College
	Waddell & Reed InvestEd www.waddell.com
Arkansas	Gift College www.thegiftplan.com
California	Golden State ScholarShare www.scholarshare.com/program_ info.html
Colorado	CollegeInvest/Scholars Choice www.scholars-choice.com
	Stable Value Plus www.collegeinvest.org
Connecticut	CHET www.aboutchet.com
Delaware	Delaware College Inv. Plan www.fidelity.com/delaware
Florida	College Investment Plan www.florida529plans.com
Georgia	Higher Education Savings Plan www.gacollegesavings.com
Hawaii	Tuitionedge www.tuitionedge.com
Idaho	Ideal www.idsaves.org
Illinois	Bright Start www.brightstartsavings.com
Indiana	CollegeChoice www.collegechoiceplan.com

Iowa	College Savings Iowa www.collegesavingsiowa.com
Kansas	Learning Quest www.learningquestsavings.com
	Schwab 529 College Savings www.schwab.com/SchwabNOW
Kentucky	Kentucky Education Savings Plan Trust www.kentuckytrust.org
Louisiana	START www.osfa.state.la.us/START.htm
Maine	NextGen www.nextgenplan.com
Maryland	College Savings Plan of Maryland www.collegesavingsmd.org
Massachusetts	U.Fund www.mefa.org
Michigan	Michigan Education Savings Plan www.misaves.com
Minnesota	Minnesota College Savings Plan www.mnsaves.org
Mississippi	Mississippi Affordable College Savings Plan www.collegesavingsms.com
Missouri	MO$T www.missourimost.org
Montana	Montana Family Education Savings Program http://montana.collegesavings.com

continued...

Pacific Funds 529 College
  Savings Plan
www.collegesavings.pacificlife.com

Nebraska   AIM
www.aiminvestments.com

College Savings Plan of Nebraska
www.planforcollegenow.com

State Farm College Savings Plan
www.statefarm.com/mutual/529.htm

TD Waterhouse
www.tdwaterhouse.com/planning/
  college/index.html

Nevada   American Skandia
www.strategicpartners.com/
  collegesavings/index.html

Columbia 529
www.columbia529.com

Strong 529 Plan
*Effective August 13, 2004, accounts in The
Strong 529 Plan were transitioned into new
accounts in the Upromise College Fund.*

Upromise College Fund
http://uii.s.upromise.com/index.html

USAA College Savings
www.lc.usaa.com

Vanguard 529
www.vanguard.com

New Hampshire	Advisor College Investing Plan www.advisorxpress.com
	Unique College Investing Plan www.fidelity.com/unique
New Jersey	New Jersey Higher Education Student Assistance Authority www.hesaa.org
	Franklin Templeton www.franklintempleton.com
New Mexico	Arrive Education Plan www.arrive529.com
	CollegeSense www.collegesense.com
	The Education's Plan's College Saving Program www.theeducationplan.com
	Scholar's Edge www.scholarsedge529.com
New York	New York's College Savings Program www.nysaves.com
North Carolina	National College Savings Program www.cfnc.org/savings
	Seligman College HorizonFunds www.seligman529.com
North Dakota	College SAVE www.collegesave4u.com

Ohio	CollegeAdvantage Savings Plan www.collegeadvantage.com
	Putnam CollegeAdvantage Savings Plan www.putnam.com
Oklahoma	Oklahoma College Savings Plan www.ok4saving.org
Oregon	MFS 529 Savings Plan www.mfs.com/college/529_plan/ index.jhtml
	Oregon College Savings Plan www.oregoncollegesavings.com
	USA Collegeconnect www.usacollegeconnect.com
Pennsylvania	TAP 529 Investment Plan www.lfg.com/lfg/pa5/index.html
Rhode Island	CollegeBoundFund www.collegeboundfund.com
	JP Morgan Higher Education Fund http://jpmorganfleming.chase.com/ mutualfunds/education/benefits.jsp
South Carolina	Future Scholar www.futurescholar.com
South Dakota	College Access 529 www.collegeaccess529.com
	Legg Mason Core4College www.leggmason.com/funds/ core4college/index.asp